Endors

"Debbie releases these timeless strategies with a unique writing style that keeps the reader engaged and captivated, walking them into total transformation."

—Kary Oberbrunner, author of *Day Job to Dream Job* and *Your Secret Name*

"For complete transformation from all obstacles, deception, and disappointments that hinder you from fulfilling your God-given assignment on earth, *Strategies from Heaven* by Debbie Bilek is the timely gift that will forever change your life."

—Dr. Bishop Hudson Suubi – Uganda Africa

Also by Debbie Bilek:

Smiling on the Outside, Dying on the Inside

Strategies from Heaven

Contending for the Impossible

DEBBIE BILEK

Published by Author Academy Elite
P.O. Box 43, Powell, OH 43065

Library of Congress Control Number: 2019913768

Softcover: 978-1-64085-926-5
Hardcover: 978-1-64085-927-2
Ebook: 978-1-64085-928-9

Available in hardcover, softcover, e-book, and audiobook.

DEDICATION

This book is dedicated to God. With You, Lord, every day is a new adventure. Thank You for choosing this broken vessel and breathing life back into me. Thank You for going into the dark places of my soul and bringing light. Thank You for Your transformative power that gives true purpose and destiny. I love You with every fiber of my being.

Your beloved daughter,
Debbie

Contents

Acknowledgments

Thank you to my faithful, loving, devoted husband of 31 years, William Bruce Bilek. This man is the most precious gift the Lord has given to me. He has stood by my side through everything. I have never had to doubt his love or devotion to me. He sees me at my worst and still chooses to love and support me, speaking life and encouragement to my soul, praying for me with everything in him. He sees me at my best and stands by my side, cheering me on as my biggest fan and most treasured friend. Thank you, my sweet and humble soul mate, for all that you are to me. I would not be the woman I am today without you, as a man, standing by my side, gently guiding and leading me in the ways of the Lord. I will love you forever.

I give thanks to two friends who have prayed for me and my family for many years. I'm not sure where I would be today without their gracious intercession. They have invested so much into our lives spiritually and in numerous other ways. I am forever grateful to Barbara Savryk and Joni White. Thank you for your selfless devotion and love. May the Lord repay you a hundredfold for all you have so freely given to the Bilek family.

I want to acknowledge and give thanks for my beta readers, Pastor Roger Williams, Addie Campbell, Sandi Redman, Ric Gahm, Shari Gahm, Victoria Mumford, and my precious baby girl, Rebekah Lynn Bilek, who graciously agreed to read over my manuscript before it went to the publishing editor. Thank you for being my extra sets of eyes. I am grateful for each of you. Your suggestions, insight, and care for detail have been invaluable contributions to the success of this book. You guys rock!

Lastly, I give thanks to my son, Brennan, who had the courage to tell me upon reading my first draft, "Mom, this book just doesn't have the impact of your last book." His comment stopped me in my tracks, made me get on my face before the Lord, put the book aside for three months, and eventually revamp the whole project. I am ever grateful for the many ways you sharpen me, Brennan Robert Bilek. You are the son every mother dreams of.

A Note to the Reader

Each year in January I sit down with God and ask Him for my assignments for the new year. This year was no different. I knew I was commissioned to write another book, but I did not yet know its content. I listened in silence. A while later I picked up my pen to begin journaling and I saw in my mind's eye three words: *Strategies from Heaven.* I wrote them down in my journal and also typed them into my phone notes. I didn't quite know what they meant but did not want to forget.

Two weeks later I attended a women's gathering to hear a special guest speaker whom I did not know. At the end of her talk, she invited anyone wanting prayer to go up to the front. I went forward with a few others, closed my eyes, and began to quietly pray. Several minutes passed by when I felt someone's hand on my shoulder. As she began praying for me, I recognized it was the voice of the speaker. She prayed a few things and then said, "I see you writing a book. I'm not sure what it's about, but I see three words: *Strategies from Heaven.*" I about passed out! I opened my eyes and blurted out, "Wait here!" I hurried over to my purse, reached in, and grabbed my phone. I ran back over to her, my heart jumping with excitement. I opened my notes and showed her what I had transcribed two weeks prior. The same three words: *Strategies from Heaven*. We both began crying. I knew my next assignment.

I encourage you to read this book with a small group of friends for accountability and to experience a deeper impact. It is always powerful to go through life with those who are not afraid to sharpen us, pull us higher, and challenge us to grow. Please refer to the *Discussion Points* at the back of this book that are intended to be used for this very purpose.

Knocking on Death's Door

Startled out of a deep sleep, I awoke wondering what caused the loud thump outside of my bedroom window. Rubbing my eyes, I dragged myself over to the window and pulled up the blind. At a glance, I could see that a large branch from the oak tree over my backyard deck had come down with a thud. I slowly crawled back into bed, feeling gloomy, as I pondered what this new day would hold. I was tired and felt a gnawing dread in the pit of my stomach. It was an overwhelming feeling that something wasn't right. Thoughts raced through my head as I replayed the previous year's events. I was in a good place. Life was going well. I had been healed of numerous autoimmune diseases and was getting my life back. I felt alive again. So where was this deep sense of despair coming from?

As I dozed in and out of sleep, my cell phone vibrated. I reached over to pick it up. I didn't recognize the number and usually wouldn't answer to an unknown caller first thing in the morning, but something inside told me I should answer. It was my doctor calling from his personal cell phone. I was startled to hear his voice. This was a man who had been instrumental in my own healing journey a few years earlier. I hadn't been to see him recently and was wondering what the call could possibly be about. His voice came across the phone a bit shaky, not like the strong man I remembered who had led me through some very difficult times. After announcing his name, he said, "I hope I'm not calling too early." I replied with a nervous "no." He went on to tell me that he was not calling as my doctor, but rather out of desperation. He knew I believed in God and that my faith was strong. We had shared numerous spiritual conversations over the past few years. He proceeded to relate the story of how his beloved wife had attempted to take her life that week. His voice was distressed as he asked me for prayer. He said, "I didn't know what else to do. I knew you would pray."

I fumbled through a prayer over the phone, feeling helpless. I sensed his desperation. He and his wife had three small children under the age of three. My heart sank. I told him I would continue to pray as I hung up the phone. I asked God if there was something I should do. I felt as if I was supposed to go over to their house, but I had only met his wife a couple of times and I didn't know if she would remember who I was. Would an unannounced visit startle her? Would it make matters worse if she found out her husband had called me, sharing her secret? Would she even recognize me or open the door?

The dread I had been feeling that morning increased. I knew I had to act. As I prayed, I felt the tugging of the Lord prompting me to go. I texted my doctor and asked him for their address. I showered, dressed, and headed out the door, prayers on my lips and Bible in hand. A nervousness arose in my heart. What if I make things worse? God began to calm me, as He brought to mind everything I had been through. I had been chronically ill for over twenty years. He reminded me of all the people He had sent my way who were instrumental in my own healing journey. As the memories flooded my mind, one after another after another, I knew I was doing the right thing. I prayed for wisdom and favor.

I parked in front of their house, wondering what on earth I would say if she opened the door. I thought, *Okay, God. I'm going to do this, but when I open my mouth, You have to fill it!* My body shook as my fist gave a gentle knock on the door. Deep inside I was secretly hoping that maybe she wouldn't answer.

The door slowly opened a crack. I saw a beautiful young woman, with eyes of despair, peeking out at me with fear and confusion. I said, "Hi. I don't know if you remember me, but I am a patient of your husband. The Lord showed me that you are carrying something too heavy for you to carry alone." Tears welled up in her eyes as she opened the door wide and motioned me to come in. Her three babies, ages three, one and a half, and three months old were lined up on the floor, as she had been changing their diapers. The youngest two were crying.

I prayed silently for something to say that would encourage her, that would let her know she had a Father in heaven who loved her and deeply cared about her every need. I relayed the events of the morning and how I had awoken with deep gloom and despair. I shared how as the hours progressed, I began to realize that the burden was not for me, but for her. Tears streamed steadily down her cheeks as she reported that the previous night she had been crying out for God to put her on someone's heart, to send someone to help her. I don't remember much of the conversation that transpired in that moment, however, I do know that I was not speaking my words, but rather the words of a Father in heaven who had orchestrated a divine appointment to bring hope and encouragement to His precious daughter who had lost all aspirations to live.

Many of you are experiencing your own internal crisis. Some are wondering if life is worth living. Others are struggling with addictions or chronic health issues that have taken you out of the game. Many of you are broke, depressed, full of anxiety, or just plain weary. Some are asking yourselves, "Why am I here? What is my purpose?" Others are dealing with relationship issues — hurting marriages and prodigal children. There is a huge identity crisis taking place in this generation regarding sexual identity.

Strategies from Heaven will impart timeless strategies that will allow you to conquer those situations where you have lost all hope. By the time you get to the last chapter you will know who you are and what you were created for. You may have been derailed, but the purpose of this book is to get you back on track. I cherish the opportunity to build your faith and instill deep hope as you *contend for the impossible*.

PART I

Created on Purpose

CHAPTER 1

Derailed

How Did I Get Here?

Cast all your anxiety on Him because He cares for you.
1 Peter 5:7

There is an enemy of our soul who comes to steal, kill, and destroy (John 10:10). The Bible refers to him as a fallen angel, Satan, and the prince of darkness. I had been one of his victims. For over twenty years I physically suffered from daily pain and chronic illness. My life had been derailed by interstitial cystitis, fibromyalgia, chronic fatigue syndrome, Hashimoto's thyroiditis, Sjögren's syndrome, migraine headaches, and reflex sympathetic dystrophy. I often wondered, *How in the world did I get here?* I believed in God and knew that He loved me but could not understand why He allowed me to suffer so terribly.

One night, as I was attempting to go to sleep but not making much progress due to the constant pain, I stared at the ten bottles of prescription medication that had taken over my nightstand. I reached for one. I opened the bottle… I closed the bottle… I opened the bottle again. I lifted it to my mouth. Something stopped me. I flung the bottle against the wall as pills scattered across the room. I was done — and I knew it. I flung my hand across the nightstand, causing the remaining nine bottles to go crashing to the floor. I rolled over, pulled the covers up tight around my neck, placed a pillow over my head, and cried myself to sleep.

I woke up the next morning and stated aloud, "Today is the day that I live or die." It was a miracle I had made it through the night. I couldn't get the thought of wanting to swallow that bottle of pills out of my head. Through a series of God interventions, I lived (as you probably guessed since you are reading my book). You can read more of my personal story in my book *Smiling on the Outside, Dying on the Inside*. My journey has been a long one — painful at times, full of life and joy at other times — but it is my journey. Each of you is on your own unique journey, and sometimes it can be lonely. At those times, it is critical that you reach out for help. As I reminisced about the years of pain and how God sent people at just the right moments to intervene, I recognized that I had been saved for a purpose.

"Today is the day that I live or die."

Many of you have been derailed and pushed off course. For some of you, your marriage is in shambles and you see no way out but divorce. Others have turned to vices to get you through the day and find yourselves addicted to drugs, alcohol, pornography, food, prescription medications, or other addictions. Some of you are tormented by severe depression and anxiety. Others have become so disillusioned with life that you have completely lost your identity, your sense of who you are. Some of you are suffering from gender identity confusion.

Some have adult children who have lost their way, and you are crying out for their return. Many of you live paycheck to paycheck, wondering if you will ever become free from debt. You know there must be more to life, but you can't seem to get your head above water.

You can't remember what it was like to run through the tall green grass, carefree and happy. You barely remember climbing that tree as a small child, all the while believing you could reach heaven. You don't remember jumping into the water, splashing with giggles of joy. You have a vague memory of riding your bicycle down empty streets, wind whipping through your hair, not a care in the world. Where did that little boy or little girl go? You are still in there! You still have those dreams and passions from childhood, but they have been buried by the confusion and pressures of the world.

Many of you believe there is no way out. Some of you believe there is a way out, but you can't quite see it. Others are burdened with the lie that what you have done is unforgiveable. You live day to day drowning in shame and guilt. Some of you believe that you are resigned to a life of hell because you were born into it. I am here to tell you that it doesn't have to be this way. You have a choice. Allow today to be the first day of the rest of your life!

It's hard for me to believe that only a few short years ago I was depressed, suicidal, and miserable, just trying to survive each day. My favorite place to be was in bed. I hated the thought of morning which brought pain and agony to my body and soul. I am a completely different person today. I wake up singing with immense joy in my heart. I can't wait to start my day and experience all the new opportunities and divine appointments that are in store for me. God has downloaded to me many strategies, through years of struggle, that I am humbled and privileged to impart to you in this book.

I urge you to stop settling for less. Don't give in to hopelessness and despair. You may have been derailed, but it is only a temporary setback. Your breakthrough is on the horizon! I know a God who says that in Him, there is no condemnation, guilt, or shame. If you don't know Him personally, I am trusting that by the time you get to the end of this book, you will have had an encounter with a personal God who loves you and is passionately pursuing you. You will be back on your own unique path of healing, wholeness, and life abundant. You will know who you are and what you were created for. That is the good news I am asking you to hold to as the pages of this book breathe life back into your soul. You, too, can experience deliverance and freedom from bondage. I am living proof, and I will share stories of other survivors who are now thriving rather than merely surviving.

Allow me to illuminate the truth of these God-given strategies into your life. They will help you to combat identity theft in your own life and in the lives of the next generation. *Strategies from Heaven* will inspire you to rise up and fight for yourself, your family, your children, and your legacy. When you discover who you are, you will be able to live out the fullness of your destiny and the call of God on your life.

What started out as a knock on a suicidal woman's door has developed into a beautiful friendship and a life changed forever. As the doctor's wife and I began meeting regularly, I imparted the strategies written in this book. I have had the privilege of watching this amazing young mother, who is also a doctor, begin to transform into the powerful woman she is destined to be. Though some of her very trying circumstances still remain — like having three small children pulling on her every moment of the day and night, extended family struggles, and the demands of keeping her practice afloat — she now walks in joy and peace, knowing she was created for something much greater than she had ever dreamed possible. Her perspective has changed. She has practical tools to implement when she feels trapped or starts heading down a wrong path. Her future is bright and she can now see it and taste it. She is walking into the fullness of what she was created for and destined to become.

The Bible says that God establishes our steps (Proverbs 16:9). As I look back over the past several years, I am in awe of my God. He used a doctor to aid in my healing process, then turned around and used me to save that doctor's very own wife. She is now living a life of freedom and passion to bring healing to everyone who crosses her path. You can't make this stuff up! Only God can orchestrate these types of miracles. This book is loaded with the miracles of a God who loves you, who is passionately calling your name. Allow Him in and begin to watch the miraculous unfold in your own life. In a few short months you will not recognize yourself, and those around you will be in awe. Put your seatbelt on and get ready for your personal transformation that will have a powerful ripple effect on every life around you!

CHAPTER 2

Delivered

Breaking the Chains

Do not let your hearts be troubled...
John 14:1

W orking quietly at my desk with the door to
my office opened, I heard the gentle sobs of a
coworker next door. We were the only two in this
upstairs portion of the building at the moment, and neither
of us liked each other very well. We had had our moments of
disagreement and not speaking kindly to each other. We had
even been called into the Chief Operation Officer's office one
day to rectify a disagreement. She asked if we were going to
be able to continue working with each other.

We were from different worlds and clashed in every way. I
knew in my heart that I should get up and go over to ask her
if everything was alright, but I didn't know if my compassion
would be well received. After a few minutes of arguing it

over with God, I got up and walked over to her. I put my hand on her shoulder and asked if I could pray for her. She broke down sobbing and told me her recent discovery. Her husband was involved in an affair with another woman. In that moment, my heart broke for her. I knew it was the heart of my Father God flooding my emotions because my flesh did not have that kind of compassion.

As I began to pray for her, I felt prompted to ask if she loved her husband and wanted to fight for her marriage. She answered "yes" to both questions. Her friends and coworkers had been telling her to "dump the loser" and get on with her life. I prayed over her, asking the Lord for wisdom. As the weeks passed, the Lord gave me Bible verses to encourage her.[1] I gave her a copy of the book *The Power of a Praying Wife*,[2] which became an invaluable resource for her. We began praying for her marriage and her husband, agreeing together, trusting that God was going to do a miracle. It was a long road of forgiveness and healing, but God was extremely gracious, as He always is when we submit to His plans and desires.

It was not an easy journey, and it included some hard work on my coworker's part, but in a year's time, she and her husband had reconciled and were living in harmony once again. This woman's marriage had been derailed, but God, in His mercy and grace, came in and broke the chains of distrust, bitterness, and unforgiveness from her life; pouring out His extreme love over a willing heart. My coworker had a choice to make.

When God breaks the chains, we are still left holding them. Picture your hands bound in chains. Then God comes in and severs the chains. You are still holding the pieces, but now in two hands. It is your choice and responsibility to drop the chains and let them go. This is a key to your freedom. Let go of the chains when God frees you. This involves letting go of anger, bitterness, fear, guilt, shame, and anything else you are holding against another person, yourself, or God. Don't keep running back to the same old patterns of survival. Don't keep beating yourself up or replaying things in your head. Drop the chains and let them go, as my coworker did. She was set free and she embraced her newfound freedom. As human beings, it is easy to quit and give up on those we love. We have all been betrayed or wounded by someone we love at one time or another in life. That is because we are human. We all make mistakes — sometimes intentionally, other times unintentionally. No matter the case, God is a God of grace. As He extends His grace to us, we must extend our grace to others. You will never regret extending grace to a human being who has wounded you, and in doing so, you will receive unexpected blessings. In my coworker's case, she got her family back and I made a new friend. The day I retired from that job I received the most beautiful bouquet of flowers from her with a card that read:

Once in a while someone comes along, someone who just naturally makes everyone feel a little happier. You've been that someone to me. You've given me a new perspective on a lot of things, including myself. There are things you've said to me I'll always remember and ways you've helped me I'll never forget. The times we spend together are always good times that leave me looking forward to the next time. So thanks for being the wonderful person you are. You're an inspiration to me, and I'm very glad and grateful that you've come into my life.

That card blew me out of the water. This came from someone who once hated me! Then I read these precious words she had handwritten inside:

Debbie, I just needed to take the time to express how much I love and appreciate you. The comfort, kind words, and prayers you shared with me over this past year are a huge reason I survived with my sanity somewhat intact. I will forever be grateful of your encouragement and the way you listened without judgment. I am so truly thankful for your friendship and support. I will miss working with you but know you are moving on to your true calling.

I can't begin to tell you the fountain of tears that poured out of me upon reading those words as I recalled how God used me, a messed-up person, to bless and change the destiny of someone who didn't even like me. Today I have pure joy as I follow this friend on social media and have the privilege of seeing pictures of her beautiful family. She is happy, fulfilled, and living out the path God has for her. Only God can orchestrate a story like that!

Through that experience I realized the importance of allowing God to move in our difficult circumstances and change our mindsets. If you do not truly surrender it all to God when He breaks the chains, every new trigger will set you off back into old patterns. Early in my healing journey, an elderly woman praying for me recited 2 Corinthians 10:4–5:

The weapons we fight with are not the weapons of the world. On the contrary, they have divine power to demolish strongholds. We demolish arguments and every pretension that sets itself up against the knowledge of God, and we take captive every thought to make it obedient to Christ.

As I went home pondering that Scripture, I acknowledged what a negative mindset I had developed through years of being surrounded by negative people. It was so extreme that if my husband was five minutes late arriving home from work, my mind had him dead on the street. I determined in my heart that it was time to begin changing my mindset to get rid of my worldly thinking. I began to utilize the weapons I was being given.

I started making a conscious effort to take every thought captive. If a thought aroused a feeling of negativity, fear, anger, anxiety, or sadness, I immediately took it captive, gave it to God, and asked Him to replace it with His truth. At first, this seemed nearly impossible. I had no idea how negative a mindset I had developed. It seemed every five minutes I was having to stop, take a thought captive, and replace it. It was hard work! But it has paid off beautifully. In time, my mind began to transform, my joy and peace returned, and my body began to heal. The results were so powerful that I even went as far as to quit watching news sources that bred fear and negativity. I stopped following people on social media if their posts brought up negativity of any form in my mind or emotions. I began looking to God, listening to His voice of reason, and constantly reading His Word of truth to replace the deep lies that had embedded themselves in my heart.

As humans, it is easy to look to others to rescue us or to save us in times of need. Thoughts of, *If only someone would help me, If only I had his or her life*, or *If only I had more money*, race through our minds at bewildering speed. Looking back over my past, whenever I was struggling or was facing an impossible situation, I would cry out to my husband or pick up the phone to mull it over with a friend. Through the years I have learned that there is only *One* who can truly save us, break the chains that bind us, deliver us, and set us free. Other humans will fall short of our expectations and what we truly need, but God never will.

On my own healing journey, God did use individuals at specific times to pray for me or to speak a timely word. The most memorable times of significant impact, however, were definitely those moments when I was so broken that I couldn't see past the tears. All I could do was cry in the secret place and allow God to swoop in with His comfort and mercy as only He can do.

Today I am praying over you that as you surrender your heart and life to God, you will experience His deep love rushing in, breaking the chains that bind you, delivering you, cutting off the lies, healing you, and setting you free. I decree, in the name and power of Jesus Christ, that you are a new creation, chosen, set apart, and consecrated for this time and place. Today you will begin experiencing Him in a new

> *...you are a new creation, chosen, set apart, and consecrated for this time and place.*

and tangible way. No matter how it looked in the past, today is a new day. Lift up your hands and tell Him you surrender. Tell Him you are sorry for any sins you have committed. Ask Him to encounter you and make all your wrongs right. It's that simple. You don't have to fix anything or make penance for all the times you messed up. Jesus already did that on the cross. Just embrace His forgiveness. It's a free gift called grace. He is washing away all your guilt, shame, and condemnation right now.

Some of you have already accepted Jesus as your Lord and Savior, but you keep messing up and can't seem to stay on course. Today is a new day. The old has passed away! I prophesy over you that you will encounter Him in a new and fresh way. This is not only about salvation. This is about transformation. Allow the Holy Spirit to transform you. Let Him start with your heart and mind. Take every thought captive if it arouses fear, stress, anxiety, anger, grief, or any other negative emotion, and give it to Jesus. Then ask Him to replace those negative feelings with His truth, with what

He says about the situation. You will be amazed as you see your life begin to change right before your eyes.

Lord, I ask for a fresh encounter for every person reading these words right now. Let them feel Your manifest presence as they close their eyes, raise their hands, and receive Your truth into their spirit. I ask that You show them who You are and what You want to be for them in this next season. Show them the plans You have for them. I decree Jeremiah 29:11 over each person reading this book: "'For I know the plans I have for you,' declares the Lord, 'plans to prosper you and not to harm you, plans to give you hope and a future.'" Father, break every chain as they surrender to You. Thank You that this is not the end but rather the beginning of an exciting adventure like no other. In Jesus' name we surrender our futures to You.

CHAPTER 3

Destined for More

Propel into the Supernatural

I can do all things through Him who strengthens me.
Philippians 4:13, ESV

I opened my front door to take my dog out to do her business. The moment I stepped onto the porch, something heavy landed on my shoulder. I screamed and swung at it with my hand. I caught the large object by surprise as it landed with a splat on the deck. Its wings were sprawled open flat on the path in front of me, and I quickly recognized that it was a bat! I screamed again and ran back into the house, leaving my dog outside to fend for herself.

Inside the safety of my home, still shaking, I thought to myself, *What in the world was that all about?* I heard the still small voice of the Holy Spirit say, "What you just experienced was to demonstrate how the enemy works. He hides in dark corners, and when your guard is down and you least expect it, he makes his move." The Lord was also quick to point out to me the power and authority I carry as a new creation and daughter of the King. He brought to memory that all I did was flick the bat off of my shoulder and it went splat to the ground, stunned and shaken. The Lord reminded me that even though the enemy lurks about seeking whom he may devour (1 Peter 5:8), we don't have to live in fear.

At times the enemy seems overwhelmingly large. He attacks your relationships, your loved ones, your health, your finances, your assignment, your dreams, your identity, and even your destiny. The Lord wants you to know that though the attacks can seem terrifying and overwhelming, God in you is bigger and can defeat anything you face — if you choose to face it with Him. The bat, though terrifying at the moment, was actually not that big, and with a simple flick of my fingers, I took him down. The Bible says we are the temple of the Holy Spirit (1 Corinthians 6:19). That means we have God living in us. When we acknowledge that truth, nothing can overtake us!

You are uniquely designed by a creator who knows the exact number of hairs on your head.

You are uniquely designed by a creator who knows the exact number of hairs on your head (Luke 12:7). He knitted you together in your mother's womb and you are fearfully and wonderfully made (Psalm 139:13–14). You were born with a deep longing and an intense desire to know this creator. Think back to when you were a child. You knew you were destined to be great, to become Superman or Wonder Woman and save the world. I'm here to tell you that there *is* a plan and *you* are a very important part of it! Only *you* can fulfill the destiny that *you* were created to fulfill. Only *you* can do what *you* were created to do.

So how do you stay on course when every time you turn around you are blasted by evil, temptation, lust, greed, hopelessness, and despair? I know exactly how you feel because I had given up to the point of not wanting to get out of bed in the morning, just wanting to die. I thought it was impossible to live the life of righteousness, joy, and peace that the Bible talks about in Romans 14:17. However, today I am a life transformed. Over the past few years, the Lord has downloaded strategies from heaven to me. They are biblical truths that, when applied to human life, have dramatic results. I have seen them breathe a hopeless life back together too many times to count — people who had given up, lost all hope, and were at the end, just like me. They are now thriving, full of life, joy, and peace. They are experiencing abundant favor, adventure, and the fulfillment they never dreamed possible. Some of the true stories sprinkled throughout this book will stretch you. Your faith will begin to arise as you are launched and propelled into the supernatural life you were created to live.

The book of Ezekiel (37:1–14) tells the powerful true story of the prophet Ezekiel speaking to the valley of dry bones, prophesying life into the bones, and watching a vast army arise. This story is so astounding that I have to recount it here:

> The hand of the Lord was on me, and he brought me out by the Spirit of the Lord and set me in the middle of a valley; it was full of bones. He led me back and forth among them, and I saw a great many bones on the floor of the valley, bones that were very dry. He asked me, "Son of man, can these bones live?"
>
> I said, "Sovereign Lord, you alone know."
>
> Then he said to me, "Prophesy to these bones and say to them, 'Dry bones, hear the word of the Lord, this is what

the Sovereign Lord says to these bones: I will make breath enter you, and you will come to life. I will attach tendons to you and make flesh come upon you and cover you with skin; I will put breath in you, and you will come to life. Then you will know that I am the Lord.'"

So I prophesied as I was commanded. And as I was prophesying, there was a noise, a rattling sound, and the bones came together, bone to bone. I looked, and tendons and flesh appeared on them and skin covered them, but there was no breath in them.

Then he said to me, "Prophesy to the breath; prophesy, son of man, and say to it, 'This is what the Sovereign Lord says: Come, breath, from the four winds and breathe into these slain, that they may live.'" So I prophesied as he commanded me, and breath entered them; they came to life and stood up on their feet — a vast army.

Wow! Wow! Wow! This is the power of the Lord Most High. He can take dry bones, breathe life into them, and raise them up to fulfill their purpose. I am here to prophesy to your dry bones... Arise! Hear the word of the Lord. Allow God to breathe life from heaven back into the dry places of your soul. I speak life abundant, health, prosperity, joy, adventure, energy, vibrancy, vitality, and hope into you. As you read these words of life, you will begin an encounter with a personal God that will change the course of your destiny forever. You are feeling strength returning to your spirit right now. Keep reading and begin implementing these strategies from heaven. You will never be the same!

PART II

Strategies from Heaven

CHAPTER 4

The Power of Your Decree

Create the World You've Always Dreamed of

You will also decree a thing, and it will be established for you;
and light will shine on your ways.
Job 22:28, NASB

Thereshe sat, behind the cold, white, sterile walls of a hospital room. She had been sentenced to isolation for a month now due to a highly contagious disease. She was lonely, depressed, very ill, and losing hope. Thoughts of never escaping this life of isolation raced through her head almost every moment of the day. How much longer could she endure the hopelessness and despair that haunted her twenty-four seven? Had it not been for the large window in her room that looked out over the beautiful hospital gardens, giving her a connection to the outside world, I think she might have not survived what turned into a very long six-month stay. Merri had been sick for most of her life. She struggled with numerous rare diseases which led to the amputation of one of her legs as a young adult. Wheelchair-bound and handicapped in many ways, she struggled through life as best she could. We watched her deteriorate from an intelligent, college instructor in her late twenties to a mentally unstable, physically deteriorating woman in her fifties. It had been a hard road. Not many doctors had the knowledge of how to treat her or what to do for her.

As my husband and I suited up with gowns and gloves in order to be allowed to visit with her, many thoughts roamed through my head. I met Merri when I was a teenager in college. She was the sister of my boyfriend, who eventually became my beloved husband. Merri and I hit it off from the start. She had such a sweet, tender spirit and was precious to me. To walk with her through the many years of deterioration was extremely painful. What could we say that would possibly cheer her up? What hope could we provide?

I sat on the bed next to her, tears streaming down her cheeks. I begged God to give me something that would cheer her up, something that would give her hope to hold on to. I began to remind Merri of the Apostle Paul, who was beaten, chained, imprisoned, and treated most unfairly. I recounted to Merri how this man, who was not handed a fair ride in life, went on to write much of the New Testament of the Bible while behind prison walls. His words have brought healing, life, salvation, and hope to more people than we will ever be able to count through the years. I began to see a spark of encouragement in Merri's eyes.

The Lord brought to mind a Bible verse I had recently memorized, Job 22:28, which says, "You will also decree a thing and it will be established for you; and light will shine on your ways" (NASB). As my husband and I began decreeing the word of God[1] over Merri, we watched in awe as a miraculous transformation began slowly occurring in her. Merri's mind and body had begun deteriorating at a rapid pace over the prior years. She was to the point of not being able to complete a logical phrase when speaking. Her voice would trail off mid-sentence until she would sheepishly reply that she couldn't remember what she was going to say. When she would ask us for a phone number of one of our siblings, she would pick up the pencil to write, her hand shaking so badly that not a single number could be read. Her vision was failing and she was unable to even read a book.

Each time we visited Merri, we determined in our hearts that God was going to heal her, just as He had healed me. We stopped listening to the reports of the doctors and began believing the report of the Lord. His report says that He died for Merri and took on all of her iniquities and healed all of her diseases (Isaiah 53:4-5). We began speaking His promises over her life through daily phone calls, notes, and letters. We lived two and a half hours away but visited as often as we could to pray for her and speak life over her.

In just a few short months we began to see incredible improvements. Merri began reading her Bible. She began speaking God's Word over her own life. Soon she was able to write. She began filling up notebook after notebook with the most beautiful handwriting. I'll never forget the day she proudly called, excited to share that she had memorized her very first Bible verse: "Now faith is confidence in what we hope for and assurance about what we do not see" (Hebrews 11:1). As Merri began speaking this verse over her life, she was walking into it! This from a woman who had been diagnosed with early onset Alzheimer's disease! The Lord was restoring to her everything the enemy had come in and stolen. We could not keep up with purchasing enough spiral bound notebooks for her to write in. One of Merri's siblings eventually purchased a laptop for her. Within months she had completed a book which contains the story of her life. We are in utter amazement at the miracle that continues to take place in Merri's mind and body. We are convinced, without a doubt, that she will walk out of her care facility someday, fully healed and restored to the life she was destined to live.

Merri has started writing her second book, a book on healing. Only God could orchestrate this miracle that no doctor had even begun to imagine. He took her life, redeemed her from the plans of the enemy, and is giving her new purpose and destiny. He restored Merri's identity. She knows who she is — a child of the living God — and is now living her life from that truth. Even though she is still residing in a long-term care facility at the time of this writing, she is no longer living as the sick, mentally and physically ill victim that the devil tried to make her believe she was. She is living as a daughter of the King, full of authority and power. She is currently applying to grad schools to obtain her doctorate degree!

Merri's testimony has given me a boldness to speak Scripture over everyone I know who is struggling. "He sent out His Word and healed them, He rescued them from the grave" (Psalm 107:20) becomes, "He sent out His Word and healed *Sue*, He rescued her from the grave." I insert names into the Scripture, believing it for the person, and speaking it out loud over them. I am activating the power of decreeing and declaring the Word of God. God spoke the world into being. He opened His mouth and stated it and it happened. "In the beginning was the Word, and the Word was with God, and the Word was God" (John 1:1). God is the Word. When we speak the Word, we activate the power of God over lives.

I am convinced that we need to begin speaking the Word of God over every area of our lives that does not align with who God says we are and His plans for us. The enemy has come in and has attempted to steal your destiny. Rise up and begin fighting back. Instead of pleading, "Please, God," like many of us do in our desperation, begin warring

> *... we need to begin speaking the Word of God over every area of our lives that does not align with who God says we are and His plans for us.*

with the authority you have been given as a son or a daughter of the Lord God! Begin decreeing out loud, inserting your name or the name of your loved one into the Scriptures. "'For I know the plans I have for Merri,' declares the Lord, 'plans to prosper her, not to harm her, plans to give her hope and a future.'"

Psalm 1:1–3 is one of my favorites that I pray almost daily over my husband:

> How blessed is my husband, Bill, who does not walk in the counsel of the wicked, nor stand in the path of sinners, nor sit in the seat of scoffers. But his delight is in the law of the Lord and in His law he meditates day and night, and he will be like a tree firmly planted by streams of water, which yields its fruit in its season, and his leaves do not wither and in whatever he does, he prospers. (NASB; paraphrased)

I have prayed that scripture over him for years and it has proven true in his life. We must recognize and understand the *power* of the Word of God. Isaiah 55:11 boasts, "So shall My Word be that goes forth out of My mouth: it shall not return unto Me void, but it shall accomplish what I please, and it shall prosper in the thing for which I sent it" (King James 2000).

My own healing began to take place several years ago as people began speaking the Word of God over me and my health situation. The Word was going out, accomplishing and prospering in the thing for which it was being sent. God's Word cannot be spoken and not do what it says it is going to do. That would be contrary to God's nature and character. He promised that His Word *would not* return void. I never understood the magnitude of this until people began speaking it over my life, my circumstances, my situation. As they spoke the Word of God over me, it began to come to fruition in my life!

This truth opened up a whole new world to me. My mind was being transformed. My view of God exploded! I knew He was so much bigger and greater than I could ever have imagined. I knew He could heal me. I knew He was a good Father, yet I never understood the power and magnitude of His Word, and I hadn't believed that He would heal *me*. All of a sudden, I was living it. As I began to partner and agree with the words being spoken over me, my heart was being healed from the inside out. As my heart was being healed, my illnesses began falling off one by one. I was a miracle in the making. You can read more of my healing testimony in my book *Smiling on the Outside, Dying on the Inside*.

So many of us have been deeply wounded in life, sometimes intentionally and other times by well-meaning individuals doing the best they know how to do. As faith-filled people began to tell me how God sees me, my identity was being restored. I was no longer seeing myself as the sick woman who was going to die an early death. As I began visualizing myself from God's truth, I began the ascent into my healing. He was undoing old mindsets, old behaviors, and old belief systems, and transforming me into the beautiful creation He had always planned for me to be.

Many of you are struggling with illness, addiction, depression, and loneliness. Some of you are too tired to fight for yourself. God is a God of mercy and compassion.

He already died for whatever it is you are struggling with. All He asks is that you believe that what He accomplished on the cross was for you. If all you have strength to do is to say *yes* and then sit in His presence, do it! As you sit, unplug yourself from all outside stimuli. Turn off the TV, stereo, and other noise. Put your phone away and be still. You will begin to hear Him speak as you declutter your mind from the constant bombardment of sound. Ask Him to talk to you. He is waiting for you with anticipation. Open your Bible. Meditate on His Word. The most prevalent way He speaks to us is through His written Word. Ask Him to teach you something new. Ask for fresh revelation regarding your situation. He longs to spend time with you. Oh, how He loves you!

Last year my friend Stuart DeVane was diagnosed with a hernia and was experiencing severe pain. He has allowed me to share with you his testimony in his own words. You will be encouraged when you read his miracle story:

> During the fall of 2018 I was diagnosed by my physician's assistant as having a hernia. An ultrasound revealed what appeared to be a large black hole. I asked the technician if there was any way the hernia could be sewed up without a mesh, and she replied there was no possible way to sew it up. Preparation began by consulting a surgeon who concurred that a mesh could be sewn from the outside or inside the hernia, but there was no way a mesh could be avoided. I had read numerous reports of people having complications from the mesh after hernia surgery and was hoping to avoid having to have a mesh placed in my body.

At this point I contacted people to pray for me. Bill and Debbie Bilek prayed for me face-to-face every week for 6 weeks, anointing me with oil, laying hands on me, speaking many healing scriptures over me and encouraging me.

On my surgery date, the surgeon shared that the procedure would require an hour or more to complete. My wife was surprised to see the surgeon after only 20 minutes. When I awoke the surgeon said he found no hernia, that no mesh was needed, and that he glued the incision he made back together!

That, my friends, is the power of the Word of God! When we speak it out, it has to come to pass. Bill and I were not the only ones praying for Stuart and we know without a doubt that God heard the many prayers going up on his behalf and healed him.

Lord, I pray that You break off all distraction and confusion from Your beloved ones who are reading these words right now. Captivate their hearts and minds to only hear Your voice and to bask in Your truth. Their circumstances may look grim, but allow them to feel Your manifest presence wrapping around them and holding them as You go to work to *fix* whatever needs fixing. I pray that the peace of God would overwhelm each heart in a tangible way right now in the name and power of Jesus. I pray that as they close their eyes to rest, they will begin to have God-dreams and God-visions. Reveal fresh revelation from heaven that will wash over their hearts and minds. Let them awaken refreshed and full of hope, because Your Word says that Your mercies are new every morning (Lamentations 3:22). Thank You for Your promises. Thank You that You are in the middle of whatever is going on right now. We love You and trust You. In Jesus' name we pray. Amen.

Strategy #1: Decree the Word of God

CHAPTER 5

Weapon of Warfare

A Key to Deliverance

Come, let us sing for joy to the Lord!
Let us shout aloud to the Rock of our salvation.
Psalm 95:1

One day, while feeling down in the dumps about a decision someone very close to me was making, I made the conscious effort to quit moping around and to get on with my life. After all, I had absolutely zero control over the person or the decisions being made. I was in a real slump and needed to pull myself out. I decided to turn on some worship music and start cleaning up the house to get my mind off of what I couldn't change or fix. The music began to instantly bless my soul as the words to the song "Defender" filled the room.

You go before I know,
that You've even gone to win my war.
And You come back with the head of my enemy,
You come back and You call it my victory.

All I did was praise.
All I did was worship.
All I did was bow down.
All I did was stay still.

Hallelujah, You have saved me.
It's so much better this way.
Hallelujah, great defender.
It's so much better Your way.

When I thought I lost me, You knew where I left me.
You reintroduced me to Your love.
You picked up all my pieces, You put me back together,
You are the defender of my heart.[1]

Soon I was actually dancing around the kitchen putting dishes away, singing out loud. This song says it all. When I choose to praise and worship, God goes to war to defend me. He is the defender of my heart.

The next song began to play. The words, "This is how I fight my battles," rang through the air over and over as I began singing "Surrounded" by Michael W. Smith.[2] I sang out at the top of my lungs, "It may look like I'm surrounded, but I'm surrounded by You." All of a sudden I heard a loud crash in the next room. I raced in and found a picture of a snake's body with a dragon head smack-dab in the middle of the floor. I thought to myself, *That's really strange. Where did that come from?* I texted my daughter, who was away at college, and asked her about the painting. She reminded me that it was a required assignment she had painted several years earlier in an art class. The assignment was to copy the image on a book cover of this Chinese dragon that was now laying in the middle of the room. She said it had been hanging on a nail behind her bedroom door for a couple of years.

I sat there in confusion. Moments earlier I had been in her room to fill the dog's water dish and there was nothing in the middle of the floor. Now this painting was lying there. If it had been hanging *behind* the door, and the door was wide open, how did it jump off of the nail from behind an open door and land over in the middle of the room? An eerie feeling began to rise up in my spirit. I decided to talk to God about it. As I asked Him to calm my heart and mind and clue me in to what had taken place, I felt Him showing me the power of our worship.

The painting jumping off the wall, coming out from behind the door, and landing in the middle of the room demonstrated to me that the enemy cannot stand to hear our worship and praise! This serpent body with the dragon head represented the enemy. The Bible, in the book of Genesis, refers to Satan as a serpent. The word "dragon," written numerous times in the King James version of the Old Testament, was portrayed as a creature to be feared. In that moment, the Lord was revealing to me the power of our worship. When we worship God, He goes to war for us and all darkness has to flee — or in this case, jump off the wall and bow to the King of Kings. The enemy cannot stand to hear the name of Jesus, and he will be revealed as he runs or bows at the feet of the King.

When we worship God, He goes to war for us and all darkness has to flee

As a person begins to worship, his whole demeanor shifts. Worship and praise push back darkness. The enemy has to flee! Satan and his cohorts cannot stand to hear the sound of worship to our God. It is a powerful weapon of warfare. When I am feeling down or the thoughts of the enemy creep in to taunt me, I crank up the volume and worship.

> Therefore, I urge you, brothers and sisters, in view of God's mercy, to offer your bodies as a living sacrifice, holy and pleasing to God — *this is your true and proper worship.* Do not conform to the pattern of this world, but be transformed by the renewing of your mind. Then you will be able to test and approve what God's will is — His good, pleasing and perfect will. (Romans 12:1–2; emphasis mine)

When we sing praise to God, it shifts something in our own mind *and* in the spiritual realm. It is an act of worship, pleasing to God. It transforms us.

I absolutely love the story in 2 Chronicles 20, where the King of Judah was in despair. He and his people were surrounded on all sides by several other nations. It looked pretty grim. There seemed to be no escape. King Jehoshaphat called the people to fast and pray and seek the Lord. The Lord answered them and said, "Do not be afraid or discouraged because of this vast multitude, for the battle is not yours, but God's" (2 Chronicles 20:15, HCSB). They were given encouragement and strategy. Jehoshaphat told the people to believe in the Lord their God:

> Then he consulted with the people and *appointed some to sing for the Lord and some to praise the splendor of His holiness.* When they went out in front of the armed forces, they kept singing; "Give thanks to the Lord, for His faithful love endures forever." The moment they began their shouts and

praises, the Lord set an ambush against the Ammonites, Moabites, and the inhabitants of Mount Seir who came to fight against Judah, and they were defeated. (2 Chronicles 20:21–23, HCSB; emphasis mine)

This is such awesome revelation! They sent the worshippers out first, on the front lines, *in front of* the armed forces! When they began their shouts and songs of praise, the Lord moved in and defeated the enemies on all sides. The soldiers never even had to lift a finger, nor a weapon, to fight! Their worship was their weapon of war! All they did was sing songs of praise to the Lord and *He* turned the enemy on themselves and *all* of the enemies were defeated.

When my youngest daughter was in high school, she was experiencing a period of being tormented by fear at night. As the Lord gave revelation, she downloaded hours and hours of worship music onto her iPod (remember those?) and played it all night long. Whenever she had the worship music playing, she did not wake up with nightmares, fear, or torment. She ended up sleeping with worship music playing through the night for several years. This was another real-life demonstration for me as to how powerful the weapon of worship is.

Many of you are going through a difficult season right now as you are reading this book. Begin singing praise to the King. If you are so distraught that you can't bring yourself to sing, turn on some worship music and let Jesus go to war for you! Soon you will find yourself rejoicing. Begin the shift! Know that your praise and worship does not fall on deaf ears. The Lord loves a heart of worship! Begin singing Scripture over your lives. It will shift everything for you! The war in the heavenlies will begin as the angel armies rush in to fight on your behalf. Begin singing this Scripture with your own tune right now:

> Sing to the Lord, all the earth; proclaim His salvation day after day. Declare His glory among the nations, His marvelous deeds among all peoples. For great is the Lord and most worthy of praise; He is to be feared above all gods. For all the gods of the nations are idols, but the Lord made the heavens. Splendor and majesty are before Him; strength and joy are in His dwelling place. Ascribe to the Lord, all you families of nations, ascribe to the Lord glory and strength. Ascribe to the Lord the glory due His name; bring an offering and come before Him. Worship the Lord in the splendor of His holiness. Tremble before Him, all the earth! The world is firmly established; it cannot be moved. Let the heavens rejoice, let the earth be glad; let them say among the nations, "The Lord reigns!" (1 Chronicles 16:23–31, HCSB)

We can sit, cry, pout, and live in fear and anxiety over our present circumstances, or we can choose to worship and praise the King of kings and Lord of lords while watching Him race to our rescue and to redeem the situation in His perfect timing. "When the enemy shall come in like a flood, the Spirit of the Lord shall lift up a standard against him" (Isaiah 59:19, KJV). Lord, do as You have promised and raise up Your standard against the enemy in our lives!

Strategy #2: Worship

CHAPTER 6

Fiery Arrows

Does God Really Hear Me?

The prayer of a righteous person is powerful and effective.
James 5:16

Last year I participated in a ten-day prayer gathering where hundreds of people came together to cry out for revival in our region, our state, our nation, and the world. It was a powerful time as believers from around the globe united in love and purpose. At one point during the conference, we received news that the United States of America had decided to engage in the war in Syria. The conference facilitator called one of my friends up on stage to pray over that region. My friend, who is from the Middle East, began praying in her native tongue. We all felt the tangible presence of the Holy Spirit fall on the room. She then began screaming out in English, with urgency to the lost, the unsaved in that region. She was shouting, "There is a God who loves you!

We call you in! We pull you in! We call you in! We pull you in!" It was a powerful moment in time, and I am getting goosebumps as I type these words and relive the memories of that experience.

The next morning the Lord woke me at 2:30 a.m. He showed me a vision of what happened at that moment in time, as five hundred people, in a small city on the central coast of California, came together to pray. As the Lord brought to memory the evening prayer, He began to pull back the veil and show me what was happening in the spirit realm. I saw my friend on that stage praying in her native tongue. As she opened her mouth, with each word, fiery arrows were being launched out of her mouth, heading straight at the bombs that had been released over Syria. The bombs were being intercepted before they hit the ground! Then I saw thousands of civilians on the ground looking up at the bombs coming their way, sheer terror on their faces! As my friend began shouting about a God who loves them and repeating over and over "We call you in! We pull you in," I saw the people on the ground, both hands in the air, raised to heaven, screaming out, "*Jesus save us!*"

Later that morning I couldn't wait to read the news report to see what had happened. I looked up a Middle Eastern news source and found that a significant number of the launched bombs had been intercepted before hitting the ground![1] That, my friends, is the power of prayer! And I know in my spirit that thousands had cried out to Jesus to save them that day.

Do you ever feel like God is a distant God who has left you to fend for yourself? Do you wonder if He really hears you when you pray? If He is truly all knowing, then do you really need to voice what you are feeling, thinking, or needing?

God is a personal God who longs for deep intimacy with His creation. Often in life we feel helpless. I have heard many well-meaning individuals say, "All we can do is pray." That never bothered me, until the Lord began showing me what we are actually doing when we pray. When we open our mouths to pray, we have the power to bind and loose things on earth. Matthew 16:19 boasts, "I will give you the keys of the kingdom of heaven; whatever you bind on earth will be bound in heaven, and whatever you loose on earth will be loosed in heaven." This is amazing to comprehend. When I call it forth on earth, it happens in heaven. Now instead of saying "All I can do is pray," I say, "Yay! Something else I get to pray about!" We should be praying *before* we do anything else, instead of trying everything else first. We have no power to fix or change our circumstances, but God has *all* power and has given us the keys to the Kingdom. What an awesome privilege to be able to partner with God and His heavenly host to shift atmospheres, to transform lives, to usher in healing and deliverance, and to call forth what is not, as if it were, and watch it become (Romans 4:17).

> *... whatever you bind on earth will be bound in heaven, and whatever you loose on earth will be loosed in heaven.*

Have you ever heard the saying "If you can see it, you can have it?" This is such a divine concept. The Lord gives us dreams and visions for the purpose of visualizing what He has for us in the future and pulling it into the present. This may be hard to wrap our heads around, but it's truth. As we read in an earlier chapter, Hebrews 11:1 says, "Now faith is confidence in what we hope for and assurance about what we do not see." We need to ask God to show us our circumstances from heaven's viewpoint. Jesus died for our sins and for our iniquities. His blood covered all. We must ask the Lord to help us see ourselves, and other people that we pray for, from His perspective. Then we can align our prayers with heaven and pull them in. This is powerful stuff!

God has been teaching me that before I pray for someone, I need to get His heart for the individual; to see the person through His eyes. We all have our earthly perspective and view of people. We come to conclusions based on looks or behaviors of any given individual. We must switch this to asking God to allow us to see people through His eyes. This has shifted everything for me. I know that every person was born with purpose and with a destiny to fulfill on this earth. Each one is precious in His sight, no matter the choices they have made or the circumstances they may find themselves in. When we view a person through heaven's lenses, we are filled with compassion. There are numerous verses in the Bible that talk about Jesus being moved by compassion, healing those who were in need. Let's start operating and praying in belief that when we pray with the heart of God, we are moving Him to act on behalf of those people and situations we are praying for.

My husband has a friend whom we have known for over thirty years. This friend was not a very kind man. For many years he went around doing as he pleased; saying whatever he felt like saying whenever he felt like saying it. Along life's road, he hurt and offended many people including his employees, customers, family members, neighbors, and anyone else who crossed his path. This man was married to a God-fearing woman who prayed for him each and every day, thinking he might never change, but not really wanting a divorce. Her days were filled with pain and anguish being married to such a cruel individual. One Sunday morning as she was getting ready for church, she noticed that her husband was showered, groomed, and dressed. She asked, "Where are you going?" He replied with a smile, "To church with you!" The wife about passed out. In their fourteen years of marriage, he had never once gone to church with her.

I tell you this true story to encourage you to *never* quit praying for those you love. This man, in my husband's words, was the "least likely" candidate for change. The drastic shift in this friend's life came that Sunday morning as he accompanied his wife to church and heard the Gospel of Jesus Christ preached for the very first time. The words penetrated to the depths of his soul. He went home pondering the transformative power of Jesus. Something in him had been shifted forever. Later that week he found himself in the pastor's office asking to be baptized, but the story doesn't end there! This man spent the next year going around to every person he could find that he had been unkind to, offended, or treated unfairly. He asked forgiveness of each one and left a trail of amazement everywhere he went. He joined the men's group at church and within two years had become a powerful leader in his church. My husband and I were in awe of the miraculous transformation in this friend that had occurred almost overnight.

Never, never give up. Never stop praying. No matter how grim the situation looks. God still does instant miracles. We have seen immediate healings and lives transformed in a moment in time. That is the power of prayer. God hears from heaven, sends angels into action to partner with those prayers, and moves mountains on our behalf. Hebrews 1:14 says, "Are not all angels ministering spirits sent to serve those who will inherit salvation?" Open your mouth to activate the angels. They are waiting for their assignment, and we see that they are activated at the voice of His Word. "Praise the LORD, YOU HIS ANGELS, you mighty ones who do His bidding, who obey His Word" (Psalm 103:20).

The Bible is full of prayers of faith, prayers of agreement, prayers of request, prayers of thanksgiving, prayers of worship, prayers of dedication, prayers of intercession, and praying in the Spirit. There is no right or wrong way to pray. It is more an attitude of the heart. In other words, you can't get it wrong. So, what are you waiting for? Just pray!

I had a friend who used to sit at her kitchen table each morning with two cups of coffee. She had a chair and a cup of coffee for herself and another for Jesus. She started each day, her chair facing the seemingly empty chair. In reality, the chair wasn't empty at all! She was sitting and talking with her Lord in a most intimate exchange. He just wants to chat with us. He longs for that personal, quality time with each of us. Today let's choose to sit in His presence and meditate on what it really means to *pray without ceasing* (1 Thessalonians 5:17). Discover true intimacy in prayer as you pour out your heart to a loving, personal God who longs to hear your voice. This is an integral strategy to come against the harassing powers of darkness. Let's begin praying as Jesus did. "Your Kingdom come, Your will be done, on earth as it is in heaven" (Matthew 6:10). Let's partner with Jesus in bringing heaven to earth.

Whatever you see that is wrong, or out of alignment with the Word of God, is an opportunity for you to step in and pray it right. Remember that God has put you there to flip it:

- Instead of praying, "Oh God, fix my wife," pray, "Thank You, God, that You are molding and shaping my wife into the mighty woman of God that You have destined her to be."

- Instead of praying, "Lord, I need more money to pay the bills and make ends meet," pray, "Thank You, God, that I am a child of the King and that You are my provider Who meets my every need. I decree that in my household there will be no lack. Thank You that we have more than enough to pay all of our bills, with an abundant overflow to bless the poor and needy in our midst. Thank You that my family is being used as a funnel of resources to bless the nations."

- Instead of praying, "God heal my body," pray, "Thank You, God, that You heal all of my diseases, that You took all of my pain and suffering when You died on the cross."

- Instead of going to an AA meeting and declaring, "Hello my name is _____ and I am an alcoholic", decree, "My name is _____ and I am a child of the King. I was created in His image. I am covered by His blood. By His stripes I am healed. Thank you, Lord, that I have been freed from all bondages of addiction and sin, and that in Christ I am a new creation. I have the mind of Christ. As I seek first the Kingdom of God and His righteousness, all these things will be added unto me."

Pray with me:

Lord, let us become a people of prayer, a people who move mountains, a people who pull down strongholds, lies, and every high thing that exalts itself against the knowledge of You (2 Corinthians 10:4–5). Let us pray with the faith of a mustard seed and trust that as we pray, You and Your angelic heavenly host, are orchestrating things on behalf of Your children. God, Your heart is *for* us, not against us. We know Your will is that we walk in Your ways all the days of our lives. We know that our prayers are aligning with Your will, so they have to come to pass. Thank You that You love us more than anyone could ever love us, and that Your heart is to heal us and set us free. We lay our lives before Your throne and say thank You, God, that You redeemed our situation when You died on the cross. Help us to see our circumstance rectified and redeemed, that we may pull it into our reality. Use us for Your glory, Lord, as we pray right that which is wrong. In Jesus' Name. Amen.

Strategy #3: Prayer

CHAPTER 7

I Can't Understand You

Revealing the Secret Language

*And pray in the Spirit on all occasions
with all kinds of prayers and requests.*
Ephesians 6:18

Praying in the Spirit is a powerful weapon of war. I remember the day I prayed in the Spirit (in tongues) for the very first time. I had been asking the Lord for the baptism of the Holy Spirit, with the evidence of tongues, that I had read about in the book of Acts. I did not understand it, nor did I fully believe He would give it to me. I think deep down, part of me was afraid of it. I had seen "those" people and the way they acted at times. I had witnessed them laughing hysterically, shrieking, shaking, falling to the ground, groaning uncontrollably, crying out, and outright causing a scene! I was very comfortable being in control of my behavior and actions. Did I really want to let go and let God? I had seen them speaking out all at once in different tongues and secretly I wanted to interrupt and yell out, "I can't understand you!" I was a prideful person who cared about what others thought of me and always tried to make a good impression. Growing up in a conservative, mainstream denomination, I was not introduced to praying in the Spirit, or in tongues, until much later in life. I am still learning daily about what it means to "Pray in the Spirit on *all occasions* with all kinds of prayers and requests" (Ephesians 6:18).

As I began to hunger and thirst for more of God, I found myself going up to the altar at conferences or church services when they would offer to pray for anyone wanting the baptism of the Holy Spirit. I felt humiliated time and time again as they would pray for me. Some would gently touch me on my head, or give me a little shove, expecting me to fall over. Some would tell me to just open my mouth and say, "dadadadada" or "babababababa." "It will come," they assured me. To my shame and embarrassment, it never did. I became more and more intimidated and sank deeper into the belief that God did not want to share this gift with me. I began thinking it was only for *some* people, *special* people.

One day my dear friend, Pastor Hudson Suubi, from Uganda, was visiting. He was preaching at my church about the glory and the anointing that come with the baptism of the Holy Spirit. He shared his testimony of how before he was baptized in the Holy Spirit, he would cling to his notes when preaching the Word of God. Knowing him personally and having seen him boldly preach the Word of God on numerous occasions, always *without* notes, I could not imagine a time that this man ever needed notes! I wanted what he had! So, there I found myself the following week, in a prayer room with two strangers, fifty miles from home, confessing to them that I wanted to be baptized in the Holy Spirit. They were the sweetest elderly couple and told me not to worry about it; that I didn't need to strive or beg or struggle for it. They prayed for me and reassured me that God would give me this gift, freely, at a time when I least expected it.

On my hour drive home, I opened my mouth to pray and out came the strangest words. It sounded like a foreign dialect from some hidden tribe unknown to mankind. I was totally caught off guard. It sounded so funny. I thought, *Really, God? Is this what speaking in tongues is? Does it have to sound so strange?* You'd think I would have been elated to have finally received this precious heavenly language. But instead, I found myself complaining to God about how it sounded! As I was around other Spirit-filled believers, I began listening to them as they prayed in tongues. It always sounded so beautiful, so eloquent, so heavenly. I was embarrassed to pray in the Spirit out loud. I am a tad embarrassed to even be mentioning this right now, and don't know why I am, but I believe that it will minister to someone reading this. I soon became a closet pray-er. I only prayed in tongues in the privacy of my own home, when no one else was around.

God is such a gracious, patient, loving Father. He must have been cracking up at me! I am cracking up right now as I think about how I wanted a gift, asked and pleaded for the gift, finally got the gift, and then was *embarrassed* to use the gift. The Lord was quietly and patiently teaching me humility. I had always been concerned with what others thought of me, to the point of wanting to choose the sound that would come out of my mouth when praying in the Spirit. Oh, what a mess I was! God was molding me and shaping me into the person He had created me to be as I was being knit together in my mother's womb. He is so beautiful to take our brokenness and make beauty from our ashes.

As I began "closet" praying in the Spirit, God began doing a miraculous work from the inside out. Romans 8:26 states, "the Spirit also helps with our infirmities: for we know not what we should pray for as we ought: but the Spirit Himself makes intercession for us with groanings which cannot be uttered" (AKJV). My "groanings," though pretty funny sounding, were actually God making intercession for me! I look back and thank God for His patience, His lovingkindness, and His intercession. I was ungrateful, disrespectful, and arrogant, yet He still chose to make intercession for me. That is the beautiful heart of the Father toward His wayward children.

My pastor, Roger Williams, explains praying in the Spirit like this:

> I heard many years ago that language is an agreement between two or more people that the sounds you make have meaning. For example, the word and sound "chair" do not have the same meaning in non-English speaking countries as it does with us. We have made an agreement as to what "chair" means. Praying in the Spirit is quite similar in that it is an agreement with God that the sounds you make have meaning. So, praying in tongues is a faith agreement between you and the Lord, a step of faith which, of course, requires participation, just as with every other gift of the Holy Spirit.[1]

In other words, we have to open our mouths and choose to make the sound. I thank God for His gentleness with me. I have seen His miraculous intervention in my life through praying in the Spirit. I am a different person than I was before being baptized in the Holy Spirit. I praise Him for His patience, His partnership, His intervention, and His

To think that when I pray in the Spirit, I am partnering with Almighty God to bring heaven to earth!

wisdom. I am convicted that we should be praying in the Spirit as much as we can. It is one thing for me to pray with my human mind, but to think that the God of the universe is making intercession for me is incomprehensible! To think that when I pray in the Spirit, I am partnering with Almighty God to bring heaven to earth!

When I picture what took place in the Book Acts, I can't help but shout!

> When the day of Pentecost came, they were all together in one place. Suddenly a sound like the blowing of a violent wind came from heaven and filled the whole house where they were sitting. They saw what seemed to be tongues of fire that separated and came to rest on each of them. All of them were filled with the Holy Spirit and began to speak in other tongues as the Spirit enabled them. (Acts 2:1–4)

This experience in the upper room changed them forever! Before they were filled with the Holy Spirit, they were huddled together in fear, hiding out, praying in the upper room behind locked doors. After they were baptized in the Holy Spirit everything changed!

Jesus had promised earlier in Acts 1:8, "But you will receive *power* when the Holy Spirit comes on you; and you will be my witnesses in Jerusalem, and in all Judea and Samaria, and to the ends of the earth." All of a sudden, things changed! After receiving the Holy Spirit, weak, cowardly Peter, who had denied the Lord three times due to fear, was transformed into a strong, *bold* preacher of the Gospel. The people who heard Peter speak were astonished at his boldness. How could Peter, who had been an uneducated fisherman, speak with such power and authority? Peter was no longer afraid of persecutions! People saw the transformation in Peter. This ordinary disciple became an extraordinary man of God:

When they saw the courage of Peter and John and realized that they were unschooled, ordinary men, they were astonished and they took note that these men had been with Jesus. (Acts 4:13)

This is the power of the baptism of the Holy Spirit and praying in tongues. When we don't know what to pray with our human minds, the Holy Spirit intercedes for us! What a concept! When I am in despair over my health, over my finances, over choices my loved ones are making, or over situations that seem hopeless; when everything in my world is spinning out of control, God knows exactly what needs to happen and partners with me to pray things right. God has it all figured out.

At this point you may be wondering, like I was, about the difference between the gift of tongues and praying in the Spirit. There is much to study and consider in regards to this differentiation, but a simple explanation that I believe to be accurate is that the gift of tongues refers to speaking in tongues for the edification of the body of Christ, in other words to encourage the church. We find this gift cited in 1 Corinthians 14 where Paul discusses the gifts of the Spirit. Used in this manner, we see that tongues must be followed by interpretation, in order to build up the entire church. This is a gift imparted by God to those He chooses.

Praying in the Spirit is something made available to everyone at all times. It does not require interpretation because it is a language given for your personal use to build you up in your spirit. Ephesians 6:18 says, "And pray in the Spirit on all occasions with all kinds of prayers and requests." As we discussed earlier in Romans 8:26, praying in the Spirit is actually the Spirit of God making intercession for us when we don't know what or how to pray.

Last weekend I attended a church service where Ashley Little, founder of *The Greater Love Ministries*, was sharing her testimony of how the Lord had saved her out of a lifestyle of drug and alcohol addiction and homosexuality. During worship, I noticed a young man behind me, bent over and crying. I went over to him and asked if I could pray for him. As I reached out to place my hand on his shoulder, he fell into me and began sobbing uncontrollably. He wreaked of alcohol and I could tell he was strung out on something. I sat there holding him in my arms, just hugging him and praying. He kept sobbing and began to cry out, "It's too hard! It's too hard!" I silently asked the Lord to give me His heart for this young man. Immediately, a picture of my dear friend's son, who was severely addicted to drugs, passed before my eyes. I embraced this stranger even tighter as the Lord showed me my friend's son — the young man I had been praying for fervently over the past couple of years. All I could think about was my beloved friend and her son as the Lord quietly whispered to me, "This is somebody's son."

I was at a loss as to how to help this individual, so I began praying in tongues. I knew that the God of heaven was looking down at this broken young man who had walked into that service off of the street. I knew that I was involved, in that moment, in a divine appointment that the Lord had set up. He placed me there to demonstrate the tangible love of Jesus. I was Jesus' hands and feet in action, speaking life and love into a broken young man. He was encountering Jesus as I held him and partnered with God in prayer. I know that his life will never be the same.

In Smith Wigglesworth's Devotional book, he writes:

> If I were to come to you right now and say, "Whatever you do, you must try to be holy," I would miss it. I would be altogether outside of God's plan. But I take the words of the epistle, which says by the Holy Spirit, "Be holy" (1 Peter 1:16). It is easy as possible to be holy, but you can never be holy by your

own efforts. God wants us to be entirely eaten up by this holy zeal for Him, so that every day we will walk in the Spirit. It is lovely to walk in the Spirit, for He will cause you to dwell in safety, to rejoice inwardly, and to praise God reverently.[2]

I believe that so many individuals who have given their lives to Jesus fail and fall prey to the same self-destructive behaviors over and over again because they are trying to get it right in their own power. This is where the baptism of the Holy Spirit comes in. We cannot be holy or strive to live a life of righteousness in our own carnal flesh. We will fail over and over again. This is why much of the church looks as sick as the rest of the world. We have strived to do it on our own. By our own strength we cannot possibly overcome the attacks of Satan over our marriages, our families, our bodies, our minds, our finances, and every other way he goes after us. Once we have received the baptism of the Holy Spirit with the evidence of tongues, it is crucial to begin praying in the Spirit on all occasions. In this way we are continually building ourselves up as the Lord Himself intercedes for us. We cannot fail when He is advocating on our behalf.

Pray with me:

Holy Spirit, teach me to partner with You in prayer. Teach me what it truly means to pray in the Spirit at all times. I am in awe of what You are doing in the spiritual realm as I take time to partner with You. Thank You that You love me so much that You intercede for me. Thank You for showing me that there is nothing more important I can be doing with my time, than to be spending it with You. I can be out there "doing," or I can be resting in Your presence, allowing *You* to do what You do best. Have Your way in each of us. Teach us what it means to partner with You in prayer, allowing You to be God over our seemingly impossible situations. Remind us that nothing is impossible with You.

If anyone reading this has not yet been baptized in the Holy Spirit and received your personal prayer language, I would like to pray for you now. This is an opportunity to receive the power and boldness that came to the apostles in the upper room. This will change your life. No longer will you strive in your flesh to get it right. God will begin to work in and through you with the anointing He will impart from heaven. It will become second nature to live a supernatural life of righteousness, peace, and joy.

Please hold your hands out in a posture to receive:
Lord God, I pray for the ones reading these words right now to receive Your gift of the baptism of the Holy Spirit. As You did for me, please do for them to an even greater degree of anointing. As they open their mouths right now, fill them with Your heavenly language and give them a personal encounter with the Living God. Thank You that You are Lord. Thank You that You intercede for us with heavenly groanings. Thank You that You do not leave us alone to fend for ourselves when we know not how to pray. Thank You that You are God and we are not. We release all of our burdens to You, and we take Your yoke, for Your yoke is easy and Your burden is light (Matt. 11:30). Thank You that You are who You say You are, and that You do what You say You do. In Jesus' name we pray. Amen.

Strategy # 4: Praying in the Spirit

CHAPTER 8

Unlock Your Destiny

The Keys of Thanksgiving

Give thanks in all circumstances...
1 Thessalonians 5:18

I turned the corner to the waiting room to await my turn for an MRI of my injured knee. It was as if I had entered the twilight zone. My heart stopped for a moment as I saw the room full of people all dressed the same. Each one had on a matching hospital gown, white with a pale blue design, complimented by light blue pajama pants. As I glanced at the stone-cold faces, I could see fear and death written on each one. I caught my breath as the memory of a movie I had seen many years ago came to mind: *The Boy in the Striped Pajamas.*[1] It was the story of a boy living in a concentration camp during the holocaust. The scene flashing through my mind was where all of the people were wearing matching pajama-like uniforms, fear all over their faces. They were being led into a large room, herded like cattle, not knowing or understanding what was ahead of them. As the scene unfolded, the viewers began to understand that these people, all wearing the same uniform, had just entered the gas chambers and were facing certain death.

As I walked further into the waiting room, I plopped myself down onto the one vacant chair between two complete strangers. I glanced at each face in the room. Not one would make eye contact with me. I sat in silence asking God, *Why am I here?* I knew that He had the power to heal me and that with just a spoken word it would happen. It was not a lack of faith. My faith was through the roof as I personally had experienced numerous miracles over the past several years, in my own life and in the lives of others. In my frustration, I decided to thank Him. I thanked Him that it was only an injured knee. Many were there awaiting their cancer diagnosis or death sentence. I thanked God that I had great insurance and would not have to pay for the entire cost of the MRI. I thanked God that I was not alone, that He was with me. As more and more gratitude began welling up in my heart, I realized that I really wasn't there for my knee, I was there on assignment. A man came in and called out my name. He took me into a small changing room adjacent to the waiting room. I was issued my "uniform" and was told to put it on and then sit in a chair and wait for my turn. As I sat back down, I determined in my heart that not one other person would walk into that room and feel the horror of what I had felt minutes earlier.

A while later, an elderly woman came around the corner. I saw the fear well up in her eyes as she looked at each of us wearing our uniform of death. I quickly blurted out,

"Welcome to the party! Don't worry, soon you, too, will get your costume!" Everyone in the room broke out in laughter. Every face of stone was instantly wearing a smile. In one moment, the entire atmosphere of fear and death had shifted. A few minutes later a father carrying a tiny boy in his arms rounded the corner. I noticed the boy's pajamas and saw the fear on his face. He was wearing his own green Ninja Turtle pajamas. I said, "Hey! Where did you get your pajamas? I want a pair like that! How come you got the cool pajamas and we all got these?" His face turned from fear into a proud smile. Others in the room began commenting on his pajamas. Soon the entire room was engaged in conversation with each other, people laughing and smiling. I watched in amazement as fear left and peace flooded in.

That, my friends, is the power of what we, as believers, carry. I didn't preach a sermon. I didn't pull out the four spiritual laws and begin reciting them while passing out tracts. I simply took the negative feeling of fear that I was experiencing and handed it to God. He took it, gave me my assignment, and then I acted on it. It's that simple. If we are truly the temple of the Holy Spirit (1 Corinthians 6:19) and we carry His presence everywhere we go, we should be shifting atmospheres of death and fear and be ushering in peace and joy.

You might be asking, "How can I be thankful at a time like this?" I get it! When we get bad news, negative emotions surge to the forefront before we even have time to think! We often feel guilty, responsible, and to blame for what is happening. I am here to tell you that is a lie of the enemy — a huge scheme of the devil to get you feeling badly so that all of your energy and time is focused on trying to "fix" things. We play over and over in our minds all the details of the past leading up to the circumstances we find ourselves in. This is exactly where Satan wants us; groveling, sulking, focusing on what we *could have* or *should have* done.

I, personally, spent far too many years focused on my illnesses, rather than living life and giving thanks for what I did have. As each new diagnosis came, I would get on the internet to research it, make note of all the possible complications and side effects, and walk further and further into each illness as I partnered with it in my mind and spent all of my energy and money on it.

The heavenly strategy is the exact opposite. I thank God for this trial and tribulation in my life. 1 Chronicles 16:34 says, "Give thanks to the Lord, for He is good; His love endures forever." Do I believe that He is good? Do I trust that His love endures forever? Yes! Then I choose to give thanks. Paul stated in 1 Thessalonians 5:18, "Give thanks in all circumstances; for this is God's will for you in Christ Jesus." Does that really say "in *all* circumstances"? Does "all" mean the good *and* the bad? Did Paul really mean to give thanks in the difficult times? Yes! Paul knew what it meant to give thanks and rejoice in the good *and* the bad. Paul was beaten, abused, falsely accused, thrown in prison, amongst other horrible things, and instead of moaning and groaning, he is depicted as singing praise and thanksgiving to God. Paul was thankful in *all* circumstances. He wrote the books of Ephesians, Philippians, Colossians, 2 Timothy, and Philemon from the floor of a prison cell.

"Give thanks in all circumstances; for this is God's will for you in Christ Jesus."

David is another beautiful example of a man who gave thanks no matter what his circumstances looked like. In the book of Psalms, we are privileged to see his transparency as he poured out his heart to God during times of extreme pain and suffering. Yet, in the same book we see his overwhelming heart of gratitude to God despite his troubles.

Jesus gave us the ultimate example of giving thanks in all things as He broke bread and gave thanks with His friends in the upper room, knowing that His agonizing death was just hours away.

God adores a heart of gratitude! If we truly believe Romans 8:28 which states, "And we know that in all things God works for the good of those who love Him, who have been called according to His purpose," then we can thank God even in the worst of circumstances. We can trust that He is working it all out for our good. When we look at the main characters in the Bible, they are often found giving thanks to God, even when everything around them appears to be in turmoil. They would not allow their faith to be shaken by their situation, hardships, troubles, or fears. They continued to operate with hearts of thankfulness, trusting that God was working behind the scenes for their benefit and for the greater good.

I remember, with tears of joy, the day I trotted up the stairs with ease carrying three bags of groceries. I opened the door to the house and yelled, "Thank You God! I love my life!" I plopped the groceries on the floor and fell to my knees weeping as I remembered the day, only one year earlier, that I had dragged myself up those very same stairs in pain and weakness, fell to the floor sobbing, and yelled out, "I hate my life!" I was ill with numerous auto-immune disorders. I had become so handicapped that even the simple task of grocery shopping had become one of my worst nightmares. One year later I was rejoicing at all the healing that had taken place in my life. I am here to encourage you to start thanking God for what He *is* doing, and to stop complaining and grumbling about what you think He is *not* doing. God is always up to something and it is always for our benefit.

Remember that most of us only see with physical eyes, but God and His angels are moving in the spiritual realm on our behalf. As I look back over all the years of sickness, all the times of hardship, all the times I was offended or hurt by others, I rejoice, knowing that God was making me mature and complete, lacking nothing (James 1:2-4).

I have started a new practice. When I receive bad news, or when something goes wrong in my life, I stop and give thanks. This may sound ludicrous to you, but God delights in a heart of thankfulness, and I tell you that it makes the enemy roar! It sabotages every scheme the devil has planned for me and my circumstance. The other day I found myself stuck in 100-degree weather in horrible traffic on an eight-lane California freeway. I started singing at the top of my lungs, "Thank You God for this traffic! Thank You for this special time with You! Thank You that You are working all things together for my good! Thank You for my vehicle that is comfortable and air conditioned!" I then went on to pray for each person in every car around me. It changed my whole attitude from, *This is horrible; I'm going to be late,* to moving mountains in the spiritual realm. I began to thank God for allowing me to impact the destiny of each driver and all of the passengers in every car around me as I prayed for them. I know that someday I am going to get to heaven and one or more of those people will run up to me and thank me for interceding for them! I also know without a doubt that angels were watching over me. You never know what kind of accident or incident I may have been saved or spared from by being detained in traffic. God knows and I trust Him with my life, with my time, and with my family.

I had two choices that day. I could have sat in my car stressed out, thinking over and over about how late I was going to be, allowing my blood pressure to rise, and imagining the worst; or I could thank the Lord, knowing and trusting that

He was taking care of things for me. "Many are the plans in a person's heart, but it is the Lord's purpose that prevails" (Proverbs 19:21). The Lord's purposes are significantly better than any dreams or plans I can concoct on my own, so I choose to surrender, knowing that if I miss my flight, receive a deadly diagnosis from a doctor, hear bad news, or don't know how I am going to pay the mortgage, I can trust that the Lord is orchestrating His purposes in my life for my benefit and for His glory.

Let's pray:

Lord, teach me to be thankful. Teach me to rejoice and to give thanks in all things, even when my world seems to be spinning out of control. Teach me to have a thankful heart amidst the tears. Make my heart well up with gratitude as I recognize that You truly are working all things for mine and my family's best interest. I love You and thank You for taking on my iniquities, my infirmities, my anxieties, and my fears; when You took the beating for me, and died a horrific death on the cross, so that I could truly live in peace and joy. I love You and am ever thankful. Help me to see with Your eyes from heaven's perspective. Help me to trust You in the midst of my crisis and fill me with Your peace. I choose to have a thankful heart. I choose Your joy and Your peace. In Jesus' name. Amen.

Strategy #5: Thanksgiving

CHAPTER 9

Wounds of Betrayal

Freedom from the Sting

*And when you stand praying, if you hold anything against
anyone, forgive them, so that your Father in heaven
may forgive you your sins.*
Mark 11:25

B etrayal is unfortunately not an uncommon part of life.
Most of us have been betrayed by someone we love at
some point in our lives. This can be one of the most
painful experiences a person has to live through. We expect
people to treat us poorly at times, but when we are betrayed
by someone we deeply love and care for, it can feel unbearable.
Not too long ago I went through one of the most difficult
seasons of my life. I experienced the most painful betrayal

of my entire adulthood. This is an excerpt from my journal that I wrote four months into the experience:

> The betrayal of a family member, close friend, or a loved one is one of the most painful experiences an individual should ever have to endure in life. Your heart is broken. Your trust is severed. It feels like all life has been sucked out of you, and your bones have been crushed beyond repair. It feels as if your heart is being ripped out of you from the inside out. Depression invades the soul and your mind becomes cloudy. You are unable to focus or see things from a clear perspective. It can take weeks, months, even years to feel healing or peace from the pain. It is as if every last breath is an intense labor trying to escape from your chest. The days are long, cold, sterile… but the nights are even longer, as you play over and over in your mind the harsh words of death that were spoken to you, over you, at you, about you. They haunt you into the wee hours of the morning. You long for sleep. You cry out to God. You feel nothing but pain. Peace has left. Joy has been stolen. The pain is unbearable. Despair invades. Your thinking becomes irrational. Will life ever be okay again?

> Betrayal can feel worse than a death. Because when someone you love dies, they are gone from the earth. When you are betrayed, however, the person is still there. They are still a part of your world. You may still have to see them, hear them, hear about them, hear from them. The wound to the heart can be devastating. Heart wounds are often worse than a bruise, beating, or cut to the body; for physical wounds to the body heal quickly. You can watch the changes to the color in your skin, the new cells replacing the damaged cells. The bleeding turns to a scab. The scab falls off. The scar forms. Then over time the scar becomes less noticeable. A wound to the heart, however, takes its toll down to the very

depths of your soul. It damages your thoughts, which in turn depletes your energy, your stamina, and everything that makes you function in a healthy manner. Only God can heal a heart wound.

By the grace of God, I made it through that season and came out even stronger than I was, but I had to make a choice. The Lord required something of me. The choice was to forgive. I had been wronged, betrayed, and severely wounded by those whom I deeply loved. It took months of daily choosing to forgive, to bless, and to release those who had hurt me. I prayed for them each day. I spoke forgiveness out loud. I blessed them. I asked the Lord to let me see them through His eyes and to bless everything they put their hands to. Through the months of tears, loneliness, and sadness, the Lord did surgery on my heart and gave me His heart for my betrayers. He also gave me a heart of repentance that I wouldn't trade for all the pain I endured. I learned what it really meant to forgive seventy times seven (Matthew 18:22), even when lies and gossip continued to circulate, even when there seemed to be no end to the slander, even when I had to face my persecutors regularly.

Psalm 4:1–3 became near and dear to my heart. I would cry out to God in the dark hours of the night with David's words,

> Answer me when I call,
> God, Who vindicates me.
> You freed me from affliction; be gracious to me and hear my prayer.
>
> How long, exalted men, will my honor be insulted?
> How long will you love what is worthless and pursue a lie?
> Know that the Lord has set apart the faithful for Himself;
> the Lord will hear when I call to Him. (HCSB)

David understood betrayal and faced it on more than one occasion. In Psalm 55:12–14, he wrote these verses that resonated with my heart and the anguish I was feeling:

> It wasn't an enemy who taunted me. If it was my enemy, filled with pride and hatred, then I could have endured it. I would have just run away. But it was you, my intimate friend – one like a brother to me. It was you, my advisor, the companion I walked with and worked with! We once had sweet fellowship with each other. We worshiped in unity as one, celebrating together with God's people. (TPT)

The reason betrayal is so painful is because it comes in like a blow from one whom you never expected, or believed, would ever betray you. David experienced the pain of the betrayal of a loved one, but he never got ahead of God, and he never gave in to the temptation to get even. David had several opportunities to get revenge, but he was a man after God's own heart and never took matters into his own hands. As he allowed God to move and have His way, God always protected David and brought him out even stronger through each betrayal he faced. David had a heart that knew how to forgive because he trusted that God knew what He was doing, no matter how difficult or painful the road became.

Forgiveness is a key to every crisis. Holding onto unforgiveness only breeds resentment and bitterness. It doesn't do a thing to the person we are refusing to forgive. It only keeps us hostage in a prison of our own mind, playing and re-playing things over and over again. Forgiveness unlocks healing. Forgiveness frees us to live out the future in freedom, knowing that no matter what our circumstances look like, we have opened the door to moving forward into a future that is full and bright. "For if you forgive other people when they sin against you, your heavenly Father will also forgive you. But if you do not forgive others their sins, your Father will not forgive your sins" (Matthew 6:14–15). Ouch! Yesterday I read this on a sign in an office I was visiting:

> The first to apologize is the bravest.
> The first to forgive is the strongest.
> The first to forget is the happiest.
> Author Unknown

I don't know whom to give credit for these words, but they are brilliant. There is such truth in that little saying. God has been motioning my heart to apologize and to ask for forgiveness *even* when I think I am right. It always takes two to mess things up. We can never place the full blame on the other person. We can't take responsibility for them, but we surely can, and must, take responsibility for our part in the conflict.

Forgiveness is a difficult thing. It is a most humbling experience to ask somebody who has wronged you to forgive you, but that is exactly what Christ calls us to do. It takes two or more parties to have conflict. We must own up to our part, repent, and leave the rest to God. He is our defender and our vindicator.

Recently I felt led to apologize to someone who, in my mind, was totally to blame. I didn't want to repent, but the Lord's conviction was so strong that I knew I had to be obedient. I went to the person and asked for her forgiveness. She put her hand up in my face, refused the apology, and spurted out some ugly words. I wanted to verbally fight back, but instead, I asked her forgiveness one last time before turning to walk away. She was rude and downright cruel to me. Instead of feeling rejection and anger, a flood of peace came over me because I knew I had been faithful, even though it was not well received. I had been obedient to God and thus had been set free. I walked away with a clean conscience and a pure heart. I blessed the person and released her to God.

Matthew 18:7 says that offenses *will* come. We can be sure of that. Satan uses the weakness and ignorance in people to offend. Ignorance allows people to speak out of a well-meaning heart or what they consider a "good idea," but that doesn't mean it's a God idea. Words spoken carelessly can become a temptation to divert the plan of God. Offenses can derail a believer from their destiny. It comes down to human understanding versus supernatural understanding. The truth is, there is absolutely no room for offense. Your faith may be tested, but you must get over offenses quickly or you will get derailed. Every offense brings an occasion to fall. Each offense can become a stumbling block if you allow it to. An offense can be anything that gets between you and God. You must not give the offender the power to steal your destiny.

I grew up learning to hold on to offenses. Negative things were spoken and repeated and stewed over. I realized I had held on to offenses my entire life. My relatives had offended me. My friends had offended me. My classmates had offended me. My coworkers had offended me. That is a part of life! People offend. What matters is what we do with the offense. It is pertinent that we learn to let go and release the offender. I had to forgive and move on. I was only hurting myself by holding onto unforgiveness. I had become captive and tripped up by the offenses I had been holding on to. I had to repent and let go of the offenses, as well as the people who had offended me. I pictured myself placing the cross between me and my offenders. Christ had died for them and for me.

I came to the realization that I was robbing myself of the anointing of God and of walking into the healing promised to me by Jesus' death and resurrection, because of the unforgiveness I was holding in my heart. My soul had become sick and polluted by bitterness and unforgiveness. As soon as I began to get my heart healed up, my body began to heal. This was a process. I asked the Lord to bring to my mind each person from my past whom I was holding unforgiveness toward. Then one by one I forgave them, pictured the cross of Jesus between us, pleaded the blood of Jesus over the offense, blessed them, and released them. God has been so gracious to forgive me over and over again. What right do I have to hold others to a different standard? My sick heart was making for a sick body. I knew that I was a daughter of the Living God, that I had sonship benefits, and that He had given me the divine nature and very essence of Himself. But I wasn't experiencing all of those promises. If I was truly a partaker of all that is mine through the risen Christ, then I had to quit entertaining offense in my mind. Offense can easily take root in a person's heart, with all the emotions that go with it. We must not allow offense to overtake us and rob us of our divine destiny.

Four years ago, I received a devastating phone call from a family member that turned my world upside down. I remember going through many different stages when I received the phone call. I first blamed myself. I then began to blame everybody else I could think of. It got pretty crazy in my head. The Lord called me on it. When I finally repented, took my eyes off of everyone else, and began working on myself, I was able to think more clearly and was set free for God to begin healing my own broken heart. Psalm 119:165 has become ever dear to me as I face future tumultuous situations. I insert my name when decreeing out loud, "Abundant peace belongs to Debbie, who loves your instruction. Nothing makes me stumble" (paraphrased). As I decree this word daily over my life, I see myself getting stronger, not so easily frazzled and tossed by the winds and offenses of life.

People will still wound us, but once we align our hearts and minds with God's truth, the wounds won't have the sting. As we pick up our shield of faith (Ephesians 6:16), the arrows and daggers that people throw our way, will bounce right off us.

Pray for God to help you release those whom you may be blaming for the situation you are currently in. I have a friend who blames her husband for their marriage struggles. I have another friend who blames her ex-husband for the rebellion of their children. Another friend blames her daughter's boyfriend for providing drugs to her daughter. I know for me, I found myself often blaming others when things were not going well in my life. As I repented and asked the Lord for His heart, everything changed. I began to see those who I viewed as "the enemy" as God sees them, and I began to love them as He loves them. Often, those who wound us are deeply wounded and broken people themselves. You've probably heard the statement, "Hurting people hurt people." Those who offend us are not the enemy. We know who the enemy is. He is the one who comes to steal, kill, and destroy (John 10:10).

If you find yourself stuck in a cycle of bitterness, anger, resentment, jealousy, or grief, command your spirit to arise in joy and peace. Don't allow your emotions to control you. Tell yourself how to feel! Speak to your spirit and command it to align with the truth of God in your heart, "for the joy of the Lord is your strength" (Nehemiah 8:10).

Remember also to always walk in grace towards one another. That grumpy cashier ringing up your groceries and throwing them into your bag may be going through a bitter divorce. That rude receptionist checking you in at the doctor's office may have recently lost her baby. The guy cutting you off in traffic on your way to work may have just been diagnosed with a serious illness. We never really know what is going on in the hearts and minds of others. I am finding it is always best to give them the benefit of the doubt. The *old* me would have griped and complained or even lashed back at them. The *new* me gives them a compliment or offers to pray for them. You never know the impact that one kind word will have on someone going through a bad season.

I have a friend who loves to share the story about the day she was super sad and barely made it to work. She had been sick with cancer, undergone treatments, lost all her hair, and was feeling lousy. She pulled herself together and made it to work, but was feeling horrible about how her hair had grown back in. She felt she was having a really bad hair day and was generally feeling pretty miserable about herself. She passed by a gentleman in the bank where she worked. He paused, looked her in the eyes and said, "Your hair is absolutely beautiful!" This man had no idea the impact of his words on my friend in that moment. His simple comment altered her entire mood. That is the heart of God. He knew my friend intimately, knew how badly she was feeling about her hair, and sent an angel of love to bless her in the very issue she was struggling with. In my friend's words, "His statement shifted my whole day."

Help us, Lord, to be atmosphere-shifters and destiny-changers. Remind us that "our struggle is not against flesh and blood, but against the rulers, against the authorities, against the powers of this dark world and against the spiritual forces of evil in the heavenly realms" (Ephesians 6:12). Help us, Lord, to forgive our betrayers, and to forgive anyone we are holding hostage in our minds over our seemingly impossible situation. We repent for not having Your heart and for walking outside of Your perfect peace. Forgive us, Lord, and give us Your mind over our difficulties. Give us Your eyes to see others how You see them. Give us Your love for those who have offended us. Lord, we lay our lives at the foot of the cross, and we plead the blood of Jesus over our dilemmas. We bless those who have persecuted us. We release them. They are Yours. Have Your way. Bring us back to the plans You have for us. Thank You for the power that is released in our lives when we choose to forgive. In Jesus' name we pray. Amen.

Strategy # 6: Forgiveness

CHAPTER 10

Covered in the Blood

Revelation-Knowledge

*How much more, then, will the blood of Christ,
who through the eternal Spirit offered Himself unblemished to God,
cleanse our consciences from acts that lead to death,
so that we may serve the living God!*
Hebrews 9:14

My dear friend, Sheri, was staying at a cabin up in the mountains for a wonderful week of vacation with extended family members. The first day there, she was out on a hike, stepped off the narrow road to allow a truck pulling a boat to pass by, twisted her ankle, and fell to the ground. She arose in terrible pain and managed to hobble back to the cabin. Through the course of the next several hours her foot swelled up and the pain became unbearable, leading to a trip to the nearest emergency room. After doctor observation and an x-ray, it was determined that she had fractured her foot. As the doctor left the room upon giving the report, she looked at her husband and said, "Whose report are we going to believe?" They agreed in that moment to not receive the doctor's report, and instead to embrace and believe the report of the Lord. Jesus said He came to deliver, heal, and set us free.

Sheri left the hospital with pain meds in hand, hobbling back to the cabin on a pair of crutches. Throughout the week she stayed in the cabin with her foot elevated, icing it as much as possible. Though the week was not spent enjoying the great outdoors with her family, she had an intimate week indoors with her healer, Jesus Christ. As everyone else was out hiking, boating, swimming, and having fun, Sheri laid back on an ottoman pleading the blood of Jesus Christ over her foot. She determined in her heart that God's Word was true, would have the final say in her life, and that at the end of the week, she would walk out of that cabin on two feet without crutches. And that is exactly what she did! To this day her foot is healthy and whole. She walks and runs on it with ease. She has no pain and full mobility. To God be the glory!

I don't think I will ever comprehend, this side of heaven, the power in the blood of Jesus and what He accomplished at the cross. The blood of Jesus covers *all*. He shed His blood willingly to cover the sins, the shortcomings, the failings, the sickness, the evil, and all of the wickedness of the earth. That is some kind of unfathomable, incomprehensible love. Everything Christ did for you at the cross completes you, makes you whole, makes you new, makes you pure, makes you clean, makes you spotless, makes you unafraid, unashamed, immovable, and unshakable. It's who you are! It's who He made you to be! Only God can take a messed up, chaotic, out of control life, and completely transform it by His blood. That is exactly what He has done for me, for you, for our spouses, for our children, and for every person who surrenders to Him. His blood offers deliverance, restoration, salvation, transformation, healing, hope, destiny, and so much more.

I once heard Bill Johnson, Senior Pastor at Bethel Church in Redding, California, speak about the power of the blood of Jesus.[1] He was teaching from the Old Testament about the Israelites. When the Israelites sinned, they had to take a pure, spotless animal and sacrifice it. There had to be innocent blood shed to atone for the sin. The incredible thing I had not taken note of before, is that only *one* animal had to be killed and sacrificed *per family*. They did not have to slaughter one lamb for dad, another for mom, and more for each child. They were only required to shed the blood of *one animal per household*. This was revelation to me! Pastor Bill went on to explain that as a parent, I have the authority to plead the blood of Jesus over my children, and over my family. My son or daughter may have sinned, but as their mom, I can step in and plead the shed blood of Jesus Christ, His finished work on the cross, over my children.

When I heard this, I couldn't wait for my husband to come home. He walked in the door and I practically pounced him with the news. I had communion all ready. The poor guy came in, hungry for dinner after a long day at work, and the table was set with those small communion cups filled with grape juice, and a tiny little cracker on each plate. His smile turned to a downward frown — but only for a second. As I began explaining to him what I had learned, his excitement began to match mine as we started praying for everything that was out of alignment with the will of God in our family. That night was the start of something we practice many evenings per week together. We plead the blood of Jesus regularly over our marriage, our children, our finances, our property, our home, our vehicles, our jobs, our ministries, and everything we lay our hands to. We have seen God's faithfulness time and time again when the enemy rises up and attempts to attack and take us out. The blood of Jesus is timeless and already did what He meant for it to do. His blood covers all.

This is a heavenly strategy that the devil cannot stand up against. When Jesus conquered sin and death on the cross, the game was changed forever. All we have to do is acknowledge what He did, thank Him for what He did, and receive this free gift. There are no tricks, no gimmicks, and no false expectations. Parents always like to tell their kids, "There is no free lunch in life," meaning nothing is free, that everything comes with a price. However, I am here to proclaim that there *is* something free, so free that it is truly incomprehensible: the free gift of salvation and eternal life! And the beauty of it all is that as a parent, I have the authority to decree it and call it forth for my family and for my entire household! Woo hoo! Can you feel my excitement? Jesus already paid the price. Thank you, Lord! "In Him we have redemption through His blood, the forgiveness of our trespasses, according to the riches of His grace" (Ephesians 1:7, ESV).

I have fond memories, as a young mom, of singing the song "Nothing but the Blood of Jesus"[2] with my youngest daughter as I tucked her in at night. At the time, they were just beautiful words with a fun tune that I loved hearing my baby girl sing. As I have grown closer to Jesus, I am in awe of the sacrifice He made for me and for you. Back then I did not understand — and my mind could not fully comprehend — the immensity of the blood of Jesus. To this day it is hard to imagine that a perfect, loving God, would send His *only* beloved Son down to earth to pay the penalty for my

Pleading the blood of Jesus is by far the most important and significant strategy of them all.

humanness, for my carnality, for my wicked heart. I am a mother of three children, and I cannot think of a single person I would sacrifice one of my beloved babies for. Yet, God, because of His immense love for me, for you, for all of the human race; sent His son out of heaven to live on earth. He suffered intense persecution, ridicule, torment, abuse, evil, and torture of every kind, ultimately ending in the most horrific death known to mankind. All for me, all for you, for anyone who will receive Him and acknowledge Him as Lord. What a mind-blowing concept! Too big for this human mind to conceive!

Do you realize that,

> Jesus became human to fully identify with us. He did this so that He could experience death and annihilate the effects of the intimidating accuser who holds against us the power of death. By embracing death, Jesus sets free those who live their entire lives in bondage to the tormenting dread of death. (Hebrews 2:14–15, TPT)

Pleading the blood of Jesus is by far the most important and significant strategy of them all; it promises to bring transformation to every broken place in your life.

Pray with me:

Lord, thank You that I have the authority and the power to plead the blood of Jesus over every crisis and to call forth the destiny that You have for me and my family. Bring my life back into alignment with Your plans and purposes to fulfill every page of my destiny that was written before I was even conceived! Lord, I will not relent until You fulfill every promise. You are God. You never fail, and You are ever faithful. Thank You that I can hold to the vision You have for my life, and that when I keep my eyes on Your truth and Your vision, nothing can get me down or defeat me. I choose today to stand on Your promises and to call them forth, by pleading the blood of Jesus over every place in my life and my household that is out of alignment. Thank You, Lord, for shedding Your blood and for dying for me and my family. In Jesus' name, I keep my eyes on You.

Strategy #7: Plead the blood of Jesus

CHAPTER 11

Is Your Family Cursed?

Unlock Blessings to the Thousandth Generation

*But from everlasting to everlasting
the Lord's love is with those who fear Him,
and His righteousness with their children's children...
Psalm 103:17*

I once heard a friend say, "My father died from a heart attack at a young age, my grandfather died of a heart attack at a young age, and my great grandfather died of a heart attack at a young age. I probably will too!" I cringed when I heard the words he confessed out of his mouth. I had learned the Biblical lesson that the power of life

_____

... what we speak, we become

_____

and death is in the tongue (Proverbs 18:21). Looking back through history, I see a common thread that what we speak, we become. What we say most often happens to us. This is a Biblical principal. We usually attract what we speak. God spoke the world into being and it was so. Our words hold power. We create our own world by what we speak.

Personally, I used to yell at my kids when I was having a migraine or was experiencing pain. They were just being normal, energetic children. Yet my level of tolerance was being affected by my physical condition, so I would yell out, "You kids are driving me crazy!" What eventually happened? I was slowly going crazy. Many a day I felt as if I was losing it mentally. As the years progressed, I knew I was going off the deep end, but I didn't know how to stop the downward spiral.

By the grace of God, I was made aware of this concept before my life had plunged completely out of control. Just five years ago I could not memorize anything, and I really felt as if I was losing my mind. I blamed my illnesses for my mental decline. As I began learning the power that my words carry and the even greater power of God's words, I determined I would memorize one Bible verse if nothing else. I began saying out loud every day, "For God has not given me the spirit of fear; but of power, and of love, and of a sound mind" (2 Timothy 1:7, AKJV, paraphrased). So what happened? As I began reciting this verse, I was soon able to memorize it. I then began to pray it over other people. God walked me into a sound mind as I decreed His Word over my life. I am now able to memorize Scripture and am walking out of all fear. I give all glory to God!

I know another family who has a saying, "All of the women in our family go crazy as they get older." I have heard numerous women in this family repeat those words, and unfortunately, I have seen many of the older women get diagnosed with dementia or Alzheimer's disease. My response is, let it stop with you! Don't speak it out and partner with it. The enemy loves nothing more than for us to verbally agree with his attack on our family blood line. It gives him full permission to swoop in and bring it to pass.

Is there such a thing as generational sin or a generational curse? What does that even mean? Can I really be cursed because of something my ancestors did hundreds of years ago? Absolutely! Exodus 20:46 talks of visiting the iniquity of the fathers on the children to the third and fourth generations:

> Do not make an idol for yourself, whether in the shape of anything in the heavens above or on the earth below or in the waters under the earth. You must not bow down to them or worship them, for I, the Lord your God, am a jealous God, punishing the children for the father's sin, to the third and fourth generations of those who hate Me, but showing faithful love to a thousand generations of those who love Me and keep my commands. (HCSB)

Graeme Walsh, Associate Director of the Santa Maria Valley Healing Rooms and Apostolic Center, writes in his workbook entitled "Generational Sin and Curses": "Curses can be consequences or results of sin (also known as iniquity) which are activated when we break God's Word or laws. If those sins are not repented of, there is a consequence. These sins can affect subsequent generations of our family."[1] Wow! As this biblical truth was revealed to me, I had to go back and ask the Lord to bring to light the sins of my ancestors. I was determined that the curse would stop with me, with my generation. When I looked back at the generational sins within my family blood line, I could see patterns of alcoholism, sexual sin, suicide, depression, anxiety, gossip, pride, and involvement with Freemasonry. I was able to visualize some of the effects of these sins trickling down through the generations. I began to confess the sins of my ancestors to the Lord and asked Him to let it stop with me and my generation.

The good news is that God is a God of grace and mercy. Did you catch Exodus 20:6 above? He shows "faithful love to a thousand generations of those who love Me and keep My commands." Thank You, Lord! Christ died for my sins and for my family's sins. I have authority as a daughter of the King to stand in the courtroom of heaven before my heavenly Father and plead innocent because of what Jesus did for me! Jesus took on *all* of my sins. Jesus took on all of my ancestor's sins when He was nailed to the cross at Calvary: "He Himself bore our sins in His body on the cross, so that we might die to sin and live for righteousness; by His wounds you have been healed" (1 Peter 2:24). If that is truly the case, then I can stand before a Holy God and all He sees is Jesus. Jesus is the ultimate sacrifice, who stands between me and the Father and vouches for my innocence, for my purity, for my righteousness. The Father only sees the Son in me.

There are numerous ways that generational curses affect our generational blood line. Some curses we might not even be aware of. I find great solace in the fact that I can confess the unknown sins to my Lord on behalf of my ancestors and break the power of them. God is the same God, yesterday, today, and forever (Hebrews 13:8). This means that there are no time constraints with God. He can go into my past and into the past of my ancestors and bring the sin to the present so that I can stand in their place. I can confess the sins of my fathers and receive ultimate forgiveness, freedom, and blessing for my children and my children's children to the thousandth generation. What a concept!

Did you hear that? We can become free from the curse. It's a free gift, available to anyone who wants it. Let sin and generational curses end with you. You have the authority to stop them in their tracks and to remove the power of the enemy from your family blood line. Do you notice a pattern of illness or sin in your family? Maybe it's cancer, diabetes, obesity, alcoholism, drug addiction, or homosexuality? Do you see something that has been carried down through the generations? Maybe it's depression, anxiety, addiction to pornography, gluttony, poverty, or getting pregnant out of wedlock. Whatever it is, Jesus holds the key to set you and your family free.

Find a quiet spot. Get on your knees and ask the Lord to forgive the sins of your ancestors. Ask the Lord to forgive and break off every word curse you have confessed knowingly or unknowingly over yourself or your family. As a child of God, you have the privilege of pleading the blood of Jesus over every sin you and your ancestors have committed. It's time to take back everything that the enemy has stolen from your family bloodline. Scripture encourages us: "No weapon that is formed against you or your family will prosper; and every tongue that accuses you in judgment you will condemn. This is the heritage of the servants of the Lord, and their vindication is from Me, declares the Lord" (Isaiah 54:17, paraphrased). Decree it out loud!

Walsh's book highlights two family bloodlines and the consequences of their choices:

> Around the beginning of the 20th century, a Mr. E.E. Winship published studies of two well-known American families of the 19th century. His findings have been featured in many publications since that date and are well worth passing on.

Max Jukes was an atheist who married a godless woman. Some 560 descendants were traced. Of these:

- 310 died as paupers.
- 150 became criminals, 7 of them murderers.
- 100 were known to be drunkards.
- More than half the women were prostitutes.
- In all, the descendants of Max Jukes cost the U.S. Government over $1,250,000 19th-century dollars.

Jonathan Edwards was a contemporary of Max Jukes. He was a committed Christian who married a godly young lady. Some 1,394 descendants were traced. Of these:

- 295 graduated from college, from whom 13 became college presidents, and 65 became professors.
- 3 were elected as United States senators, 3 as state governors, and others sent as ministers to foreign countries.
- 30 were judges.
- 100 were lawyers, one the dean of an outstanding law school.
- 56 practiced as physicians, one was the dean of a medical school.
- 75 became officers in the Army and Navy.
- 100 became well known missionaries, preachers, and prominent authors.
- 80 held some sort of public office, of whom 3 were mayors of large cities.
- One was the controller of the U.S. Treasury, another a Vice-President of the United States.
- Not one of the descendants of the Edwards family was a liability to the government.[2]

Those are some amazing statistics. What kind of legacy do you want to leave? One that is cursed and takes from society? Or one that is a blessing to society? For more information, or to go deeper with this topic, refer to the notes section in the back of this book for suggested reading.[3]

Let's pray:

Lord, I come before You and acknowledge that You are my Lord and Savior. I thank You for dying on the cross for my sins and for the sins of my ancestors. I repent for and renounce the sins and curses of my family blood line. Thank You that You exchanged the curses for blessings when You died on the cross.

I decree and declare freedom for my children and my children's children for generations to come. I break off every curse, known and unknown, and I decree that my descendants will walk in the blessings of the Lord to the thousandth generation per Your Word. In the name of Jesus Christ, my Lord! Amen.

Strategy #8: Break off generational sin and curses

CHAPTER 12

Secret Weapons

Oil and Cloth

Is anyone among you sick?
Let them call the elders of the church to pray over them
and anoint them with oil in the name of the Lord.
James 5:14

I attended a conference of a traveling, prophetic, healing evangelist several years ago. During the conference, people were going up to the front of the room and throwing their jackets, scarves, gloves, and other articles of clothing onto the stage. The stage became so full of garments that the evangelist had to keep pushing them over with his feet so he could maneuver around the stage. I thought to myself, *This is the strangest thing ever!* I asked my friend what it was all about. She told me that the evangelist and his team would pray over the clothing. Then the individuals would take their items home and place them on their sick relatives or friends and believe for their healing.

The next morning, I opened my Bible and began to search the Scriptures. I was amazed at what I found. In Acts 19:11–12 it is recorded that "God was performing extraordinary miracles by Paul's hands, so that even facecloths or aprons that had touched his skin were brought to the sick, and the diseases left them, and the evil spirits came out of them" (CSB). I began pondering the significance of this. If I am a disciple of Jesus and I am supposed to be doing greater things than even He did when He was on earth (John 14:12), then this was another strategy from heaven I should be implementing. The Lord brought to mind the woman mentioned in Matthew 9:20–22 who had been bleeding for twelve long years. She pressed through the huge crowds and managed to touch the hem of Jesus' cloak, believing this simple contact would heal her. Jesus responded telling her, "Your faith has made you well." It's not the cloth or garment that does the healing. It is the Lord Jesus Christ through our simple act of faith.

I decided to begin putting this strategy into practice. I began anointing handkerchiefs and pieces of fabric with anointing oil and praying over them. Whenever my adult children would come home for a visit, I would place one of these in their pillowcase. (Don't tell them about my secret weapon!) I ask the Lord to heal and to bring into alignment any place in their lives that is not in His perfect will. I also pray that He would give them dreams and visions from heaven while they sleep on that pillow with the secret weapon inside. I have been amazed at the things that have been brought to light over the years and the revelation they are receiving from the Lord.

A couple of years ago a few friends and I were asked to speak and minister to a group of women in a town two hours away. We decided to take some cloths that we had been anointing and praying over for an upcoming conference we were to host. We distributed a cloth to each person as a gift and explained what to do with them. About a month later we received a call from the leader of this group. She recounted a testimony about one of their ladies who had been struggling with severe pain in her abdomen. They remembered the prayer cloths and laid one over her stomach. She was instantly healed! This is not magic or hocus pocus. It's not a system, but a point of contact. This is a biblical concept that we have the power and authority to implement. If you are unable to physically go and pray for someone, anoint and pray over a handkerchief or piece of cloth and send it by mail. If your marriage is struggling, anoint, pray over, and place a handkerchief inside of your spouse's pillowcase and watch God move. Do the same for your rebellious child. We have to quit putting God in a box. There are no formulas or steps to follow. It is up to God whether or not He heals, delivers, and restores the person or the situation. We just need to be obedient to pray and do that which we know to do in faith. The rest is up to God.

There are no formulas or steps to follow.

There are numerous verses in the Bible that talk about anointing oil. Mark 6:13 states, "They drove out many demons and anointed many sick people with oil and healed them." In the Old Testament, God ordained anointing oil to bless His people. I recently read an article by Pastor Joseph Prince which describes how the anointing oil speaks of Christ and His finished work:

> Olive oil comes from the olive fruit. But when you press the fruit real hard, you won't find oil, only a white sap. Also, the fruit tastes very bitter. To get the oil, the fruit and its seed have to be crushed by a great weight in an olive press. The

crushing also removes the bitterness. In the same manner, Jesus was crushed under the burden and weight of our sins and under the judgment of a holy God. He was crushed to become the anointing oil that heals us today.

God is bringing the church to a place where we see the importance of the holy anointing oil. God's way is always for us to act on what we can do in the natural, and He will accomplish in the supernatural what we cannot. Using the anointing oil is biblical and ordained by God. So don't let people tell you that you are superstitious for using the anointing oil.[1]

James 5:14 boldly proclaims, "Is anyone among you sick? Let them call the elders of the church to pray over them and anoint them with oil in the name of the Lord. And the prayer offered in faith will make the sick person well; the Lord will raise them up. If they have sinned, they will be forgiven." This is a biblical concept. It isn't the oil that does the healing. James says it is the prayer of faith that will save the sick, and *the Lord* will raise them up. I want to take every tool the Lord is giving me and begin implementing it all for His glory in people's lives. God is releasing keys to the Kingdom and strategy in this new season. Let's embrace all that He has for us with an open heart.

A couple of years ago my husband stated that he was going to go out and walk the property lines. I had never heard him say that before and asked him what he meant. He said he was going to walk around the perimeter of our property checking all fencing and posts to make sure no repairs were needed. I stopped him on his way out the door and handed him a bottle of anointing oil and asked him to pray and anoint the fence posts as he walked. I anointed his shoes with oil and decreed Joshua 1:3 over him: "I have given you every place where the sole of your foot will tread" (BSB) and 1 Kings 5:4: "But now the Lord my God has given me peace on every side; I have no enemies, and all is well" (NLT). Both of these verses have come to pass in our lives.

A friend of mine was experiencing numerous nightmares, as were her children. I encouraged her to go through her house and anoint her windows and doorposts with oil while welcoming angelic presence and commanding all demonic presence to go in the name of Jesus. She took the little bottle of oil and walked through her home praying in each room. She made a cross with the oil over each window and door of her home. The nightmares subsided soon after she did this. This testimony reminded me of the story of Passover in the Old Testament where the Lord told the Israelites to take the blood of a lamb and place it over the sides and tops of the doorframes of their houses. The Israelites were in bondage and the Lord was going to deliver them from the hand of their enemy. He said,

> On that same night I will pass through Egypt and strike down every firstborn of both people and animals, and I will bring judgment on all the gods of Egypt. I am the Lord. The blood will be a sign for you on the houses where you are, and when I see the blood, I will pass over you. No destructive plague will touch you when I strike Egypt. (Exodus 12:12–13)

Throughout history we see God using miraculous intervention to save His people. Anointing your home, your family members, and your property lines is a powerful biblical strategy to implement when the enemy attempts to attack your household.

Some of you may be asking where to find anointing oil. You may purchase online or make your own. See the notes section for this chapter at the end of the book for a recipe.[2]

Pray with me:

Lord, thank You for Your wisdom. Thank You for revelation. Thank You for keys that unlock spiritual truths. Thank You for sharing Your heart, Your love, Your peace, and Your joy with us. Thank You that You don't leave us to wallow in our humanness, but You reach out of heaven with Your precious gifts and strategy. Thank You for blessing us with hope. Thank You for the tools You give us to bring healing, deliverance, and restoration to a lost generation. Thank You for choosing to use us, in our brokenness, to be vessels of love to those who need You. May we never take for granted the high calling You have placed in each one of us. May we be faithful to the call. We love You and praise Your name. Amen.

Strategy #9: Anointing Oil and Prayer Cloths

CHAPTER 13

I'm So Hungry

Break Through to Your Victory!

Even now, declares the Lord, return to Me with all your heart,
with fasting and weeping and mourning.
Joel 2:12

T he father was helpless. He was desperate. He did not know what to do. His young son suffered from epilepsy. He was beside himself as he had to watch his little boy suffer day after day with horrible seizures. The seizures were so forceful and severe that they would often throw the child into the fire where the family cooked their food. Other times he would be thrown into the river. Can you imagine the desperation? This boy must have been covered with burn marks. He must have been traumatized from the near drowning experiences. The father came begging at Jesus' feet, "Lord, please show Your tender mercy toward my son." (Matthew 17:15, TPT). Jesus told the father to bring the boy to Him, then "Jesus rebuked the demon and it came out of him and the boy was instantly healed!" (Matthew 17:18, TPT).

Later in this passage we see the disciples asking Jesus in private why they had not been able to help the boy. They had performed many other miracles and were confidently operating under the authority given to them by Jesus. We read Jesus' response in Matthew 17:20–21,

> It was because of your lack of faith. I promise you. If you have faith inside of you no bigger than the size of a small mustard seed, you can say to this mountain, "Move away from here and go over there," and you will see it move! There is nothing you couldn't do! But this kind of demon is cast out only through prayer and fasting. (TPT)

Wow! Do you long for the faith to move mountains? I know I do. I say that I do, but am I willing to sacrifice? This is by far the most difficult chapter I will write in this book. I have started it and deleted it numerous times. The Lord keeps convicting me as to what a powerful tool fasting is. I keep trying to convince Him that it doesn't really need to be in this book! Yet, God always wins, so here is my humble attempt to write this chapter extending God's heart for the spiritual implications behind fasting as a heavenly strategy.

For me, fasting is probably one of the hardest things I have tried to implement in my spiritual journey. I have cried out to God each time I fail, "I can't do it!" You see, I need food! And the minute I try to go without it, I become irritable, tired, cranky, queasy, shaky, grouchy, and downright unpleasant to be around. I have heard of people who have done 40-day water only fasts and I think they must be superhuman. I can barely fast one meal without complaining. I understand that some people cannot fast due to health conditions and I totally respect that. That was always my excuse. But now that the

Lord has been healing me up, that no longer works for me. For those who have health conditions in which fasting would truly harm you, I challenge you to look at fasting something other than food, something that you are very fond of. I have friends who take an extended leave from social media to draw closer to God. Others may choose to give up something they are addicted to, like sugar, caffeine, or television, for an extended period of time. God will honor everything we choose to give up in a fast consecrated to Him.

Why fast? There are many biblical examples of fasting in order to hear from God or receive breakthrough. One of my favorites was touched on in the first chapter of this book when writing about Jehoshaphat. In 2 Chronicles 20, we see that King Jehoshaphat was surrounded by enemies on all sides. Beginning in verse two, the account reads:

> People came and told Jehoshaphat, "A vast multitude from beyond the Dead Sea and from Edom has come to fight against you; they are already in Hazazon-tamar." Jehoshaphat was afraid, so he resolved to seek the Lord. So *he proclaimed a fast for all Judah,* who gathered to seek the Lord. They even came from all the cities of Judah to seek Him. (HSCB; emphasis mine)

Just picture it. Can you imagine several nations coming against the United States of America? As we see them coming, our President calls for a fast, and the whole nation fasts and seeks the Lord! Wouldn't that be an awesome sight? As we read in this biblical account, you can't go wrong when your whole nation comes before God and sacrifices. God intervened, caused confusion, and turned the enemies of Judah against each other! Such powerful intervention, released through fasting, prayer, and worship.

Another favorite biblical account is that of Queen Esther. If you have never read or studied the book of Esther, give yourself a treat this week. This story is the fabulous narration of how a Jewish orphan girl, raised by her cousin, finds miraculous favor from the Lord, becomes queen, and ultimately saves her nation from a thick plot to abolish the Jewish race from the face of the earth.

We find the account of the supernatural weapon used in Esther 4:16. Esther says to her cousin, "Go and assemble all of the Jews who can be found in Susa and fast for me. Don't eat or drink for three days, night and day... I will go to the king even if it is against the law. If I perish, I perish" (HCSB). On the third day we learn that as Esther stood before the king, he extended his golden scepter toward her. She approached and touched the tip of the scepter. "'What is it, Queen Esther?' the king asked her, 'whatever you want, even to half the kingdom, will be given to you'" (Esther 5:3, HCSB).

This is an incredible story of bravery, sacrifice, and mercy. Esther knew what she was up against. She knew that if she went and stood before the king without an invitation, she would be killed if he did not extend his scepter toward her. She risked everything with her selfless sacrifice to save her people from extinction. Esther knew that she could not do this in her own power. She called for all of the people in her region to fast. God honored their sacrifice, and her leadership, and intervened.

Are you up against something that is so big that you have thoughts that death would be better than living? Are you ready to throw in the towel on your marriage? Have you been diagnosed with a chronic or terminal illness? Are you pressing in for the return of your prodigal child? Are you questioning your sexual identity? Have you been overcome by an addiction that has taken you captive? Don't give up! The Lord has the answer to every problem

> *Your fast is a holy, pleasing fragrance sent up to the Lord.*

you are encountering, but sometimes He requires a sacrifice. Choose something to offer up to Him and watch as you receive your breakthrough. Your fast is a holy, pleasing fragrance sent up to the Lord. He looks at what you give up for Him, as a beautiful aroma. He honors your offering of love.

Do you find yourself in the same situation time and time again? Are you unable to break your addiction? Do you end up in the same unhealthy relationship over and over again? Have you been contending for your healing to no avail? Then you are in need of a breakthrough. This may be the perfect time to implement a fast. Offer something to the Lord that would be truly difficult for you to give up. Commit to abstaining from it for an extended period of time in humility to the Lord. Each time you are tempted to eat — or to do whatever it is from which you choose to fast — spend that time pressing into Jesus in deep prayer. The temptation will be there to break the fast, so only He can fill the void. Ask Him for the grace to fast. Watch and be amazed as the Lord rushes in to set you free from your torment, just as He did with the boy suffering from seizures.

Many of the great healing evangelists and revivalists implemented an extended fast before their ministries actually took off and exploded. Their breakthrough occurred after their sacrifice and offering to the Lord. God loves our sacrifices, however large or small. It isn't about the act. It isn't even about whether or not you are successful in what you set out to do. It is rather about the heart. He knows your heart.

You may have heard about the infamous Daniel Fast, but some of you may not know exactly where this term came from. In the Bible, we read about a brave young man by the name of Daniel who fasted on at least two different occasions with dramatic results. In Daniel 1, we see that Daniel and his three faithful friends were selected to train to serve in the king's palace. Daniel and his friends chose to turn down the king's choice food, eat only vegetables, and drink only water for ten days. At the end of the ten days we discover that,

> God gave these four young men knowledge and understanding in every kind of literature and wisdom. Daniel also understood visions and dreams of every kind. At the end of the time that the king had said to present them, the chief official presented them to Nebuchadnezzar. The king interviewed them, and among all of them, no one was found equal to Daniel, Hananiah, Mishael, and Azariah. So they began to serve in the king's court. In every matter of wisdom and understanding that the king consulted them about, he found them ten times better than all the diviner-priests and mediums in his entire kingdom. (1:17–20, HCSB)

Daniel and his friends chose not to defile themselves with the king's food or with the wine he drank, and the Lord honored their decision and sacrifice. Their fast from choice food for the ten days of training made them stand far above any others in the kingdom. In fact, they were found *ten times better* in every matter of wisdom and understanding!

Later in Daniel 10, we read another encounter of Daniel fasting for three weeks. On the twenty first day, an angel of the Lord appeared to Daniel: "'Don't be afraid, Daniel', he said to me, 'for from the first day that you purposed to understand and to humble yourself before your God, your prayers were heard. I have come because of your prayers'" (Daniel 10:12, HCSB). We can hear God more clearly when we fast and pray. Miracles happen. God moves. Ask God to move the mountains of your circumstances as you implement a fast and pray.

Pray with me:

Lord, I want to be obedient. I am seeking breakthrough from this crisis that I find myself facing. Please show me if You would have me fast for my situation, and if so, what exactly You would like me to abstain from. How long of a fast would You call me to? You are God and You know me better than anyone. Thank You that You love me intimately and that You desire to spend time with me in the secret place. Please give me the grace to fast for my breakthrough. All glory and honor belong to You all the days of my life. In Jesus' name I pray. Amen.

Strategy #10: Fasting

CHAPTER 14

I Can't Afford To

You Can't Afford Not To!

*And my God will meet all your needs according
to the riches of His glory in Christ Jesus.
Philippians 4:19*

It was a Tuesday morning and I sat down at my desk to pay the bills. As I picked up the pen to write out the usual check for $50 to support an orphan girl in Africa, I heard the still small voice of the Lord telling me to give more. I began the argument in my head responding to God: *Lord, You know that I have two kids in college and their next tuition payment of $4,200.00 is due on Friday* (as if God didn't know that!). *How much exactly were You thinking?* I about passed out as I clearly heard *$1,500 dollars*. The argument continued: *Okay, God, but is that on top of the $50 dollars, or can I subtract that?* As I heard that last thought, I recognized how ridiculous my question must have sounded and thanked

Him for always being so patient with me. I made the check out for $1,550.00, placed it in an envelope, sealed the envelope, addressed the envelope, and said a prayer. I was nervous about telling my husband what I had done. I was not working at the time and finances were tight, yet I knew in my heart that I had to be obedient to God.

The next few days were a bit rough emotionally as I wasn't used to keeping things from my husband but hadn't yet found the right moment to break the news to him. Friday rolled around and I still hadn't told him about the money I had given away. He came home from work and handed me his paycheck with a funny grin on his face. I opened it up and saw that he had received an unexpected $6,000.00 bonus. I about passed out! As we sat down for dinner, I recounted to him what had occurred on Tuesday, confessed, and apologized for not telling him sooner. We rejoiced at God's faithfulness. He not only gave us the college tuition amount that was due, but he gave us extra money to give back to Him for His Kingdom purposes. God had just demonstrated His overwhelming love and faithfulness. I was learning another biblical strategy: that a person cannot out-give God.

Malachi 3:10 boasts, "'Bring the whole tithe into the storehouse, that there may be food in My house. Test Me in this,' says the Lord Almighty, 'and see if I will not throw open the floodgates of heaven and pour out so much blessing that there will not be room enough to store it.'" My husband and I had always been regular tithers, but this miracle shifted something in my perspective. That day I determined that I wanted to become radically generous. I asked the Lord to turn me into not just a radical giver but one who gives with pure joy.

Two months later I received an email from the founder of the orphanage that we had been supporting in Africa. He was thanking us for the timely financial gift. His father had passed away. Being the extremely influential leader that he is, the whole region had come out for his father's memorial service. He told us that the donation had covered the entire cost of the funeral and fed every guest! That, my friends, is the power of being in tune with the voice of the Lord and responding with our humble *yes*. God was orchestrating a miracle behind the scenes to make provision for His servant in Africa and to teach His daughter in the United States of America a massive lesson in obedience that shot my faith through the roof.

As children of God, we have all access to His heavenly resources.

As children of God, we have all access to His heavenly resources. Matthew 6:33 says, "But seek first the Kingdom of God and His righteousness, and all these things will be given to you as well." Does this scripture say that *some* things will be given to us? No! It says *all* things. "All things" signifies *everything* we need. As children of the King and heirs to the throne, God will provide for and meet our every need. We will never be in want or lack. That is what His Word says, so why are so many believers experiencing devastating financial struggles?

Whenever somebody asks me to pray for a financial issue, one of the first questions I ask them is whether or not they tithe. Usually the answer goes something like this: "Well, not regularly" or "I give when I can" or "I want to but there isn't anything left after paying the bills." It is important that we understand Kingdom living when discussing tithing. Kingdom thinking is upside down compared to how most of the world lives:

- The world says to stress out. Jesus says, "Peace I leave with you" (John 14:27).

- The world says to pay your bills and then use the rest of your money on whatever you desire (that is, if there is any money left over). God says, "'Bring the whole tithe into the storehouse, that there may be food in my house. Test me in this,' says the Lord Almighty, 'and see if I will not throw open the floodgates of heaven and pour out so much blessing that there will not be room enough to store it'" (Malachi 3:10).

- The world says to scream, shout, cuss, and get revenge. God says, "Be kind to one another, tenderhearted, forgiving one another, as God in Christ forgave you" (Ephesians 4:32, ESV).

- The world says to cry, pout, have anxiety, and be depressed when we face a crisis. God says to rejoice always (Philippians 4:4) and "Give thanks in all circumstances..." (1 Thessalonians 5:18).

- The world says, "I'm an alcoholic," "I'm gay and was born this way," "My father died young, I guess I will too." Christ says, "For we know that our old self was crucified with Him so that the body ruled by sin might be done away with, that we should no longer be slaves to sin" (Romans 6:6, NIV). "But you are a chosen people, a royal priesthood, a holy nation, God's special possession, that you may declare the praises of Him who called you out of darkness into His wonderful light" (1 Peter 2:9).

- The world says, "I have no choice," "I am at their mercy," "Whatever happens, happens." The Bible says, "The steps of the righteous are ordered by the Lord" (Psalm 37:23, KJV).

Looking at this list, God's way seems to have a much better outcome. It may go against our fleshly nature, but the more time we spend with Him, and the more we begin to implement His strategies, the more we begin to see with spiritual eyes. Peace floods our souls in even the most chaotic of situations. We begin to live that supernatural life that we read about in the Bible.

Now let's look at the financial application to this upside-down thinking. Have you ever known those people with the biggest, most generous hearts? They seem to never be without. They give and they give and they keep getting more. Well, this is because they understand and implement the biblical strategy of Kingdom finances. They have become the funnel for God to flow through. You truly cannot out-give God. This is a strategy you can begin immediately implementing even when you think there is nothing to give. You will experience the miraculous in your own life as you begin breaking off the chains of poverty and lack that have bound you through the generations. Once we realize and acknowledge that everything we have belongs to the Lord, it makes it very easy to release it and give it back with a joyful heart.

My husband and I sat on the couch last weekend reminiscing, as our youngest is about to graduate from college next month. We rejoiced with thankful hearts as we sent off our last college tuition payment. It was a bittersweet moment in time as we pondered the faithfulness of the Lord. Ten years ago, we sent our oldest child off to a private university. Three years later, our second child went off to a private university. Three years after that, our youngest child also decided to attend a private university. Looking back, over the years, we stand in awe of our God, who has been our most faithful provider. Logically speaking, if we were to write out our budget over the past ten years on paper, it would not add up. Most of those years, I was only able to work part time, if at all, due to chronic illness. Yet, we never missed a payment and are coming out the other side debt-free. Only God could pull off a miracle like that! Private school tuition for three children on mostly one income over ten years, with thousands of dollars in medical bills going out each year. Only God!

I do not write to boast. This has nothing to do with my husband and me. This has everything to do with God's Word and His truth. As we are faithful to give to God first, He has always been faithful to meet our every need. If we had waited to give to God after paying all of the bills, there would never have been anything left. It is a total trust thing. Do I believe the Word of God? Do I step out in faith to give of my first fruits? Yes! And when I do, there is always enough, never a lack. It boils down to this question. Can I afford to give? The answer: I can't afford not to!

I had the privilege of spending this past weekend with my beloved 102-year-old grandmother, my abuelita. She is struggling in many ways, but God was faithful to give us precious time of reminiscing, laughing, and praying together. As I watch my abuelita's body and mind deteriorate physically, I find solace in knowing that soon she will be in paradise with my heavenly Father and many loved ones who have gone before her.

As I walked through her home, the house that many in my family helped to build, I couldn't help but weep. So many treasured memories in that house. My grandparents immigrated from Mexico and knew what poverty was. My mother remembers, as a child, following the wealthy kids to school and picking up the orange peels that they were dropping to the ground. She would eat them in order to ease her hunger pains within. As I walked from room to room, knowing full well that it might be the very last time I ever walked through that house again, my mind raced with memories and an array of emotions flooded my heart. My grandparents truly lived the American Dream. They came to the United States of America when my mother was just ten years old. They worked hard, saved their money, and purchased a home. The home was empty at first, but they had four walls and a roof over their heads. They struggled and suffered and many times went without.

The years of sacrifice and hard work paid off as they retired in Southern California. They purchased their dream of owning their own piece of property. They built the home that they would live out the rest of their years in, on that beautiful one-acre parcel. My grandfather, Tata, passed away two years ago, just shy of his 104th birthday. Oh, the things my grandparents must have seen and experienced through the years!

I walked through the house looking at the furniture, the pictures, the treasures, and all the things that one usually finds in a Mexican-American home in the United States of America, and my heart became sad. So many memories of making tortillas and tamales in that little kitchen with Abuelita or watching western movies in the living room with Tata. I reminisced about riding the little tractor through the property, picking oranges, lemons, pumpkins, and figs, or running around with my cousins and having slumber parties with our beloved grandparents. Abuelita always welcomed us with treats, as she sat on the couch crocheting blankets for each of us. Oh, the laughter and the tears our family has shared in that little home. I remember holding up two-by-fours while my dad, my uncles, and my grandfather constructed the walls. We all helped in some small way to build that beautiful little Spanish style casita with the white arches in front. We were so proud of our special ranchita that we came to love and cherish.

While reminiscing through the years, one thought played over and over in my mind: It doesn't boil down to what you have acquired. You can't take any of it with you. My mom and her siblings have to decide soon what to do with all the stuff. There are three options: sell, give away, or throw away. The Lord brought to mind how often we strive for things — for the next new toy, appliance, piece of furniture, vehicle, television, house, cell phone, computer, etc. In the end, it all gets left behind. I thought about the years I had spent striving, pursuing "things" rather than the heart of God. My Father in heaven was gently reminding me, through my grandmother's aging process, that the only thing we can take with us when we die is other people. All the years we strive for that next promotion, that next desire; none of it matters in the end. The only thing that truly matters is who I shared the love of Jesus with. John 3:3 says, "Very truly I tell you, no one can see the kingdom of God unless they are born again."

How many people did I pass by and not stop to share the love of Jesus with? How many years did I spend being about my own business, rather than being about His business? I remember being at the bedside of a dying friend a few years ago. In that tender moment, as she was passing from earth to eternity, she spoke out, "None of it matters. It just doesn't matter." I believe that as she was seeing the face of Jesus, she was trying to give us a message. All of the things we consume ourselves with, all of the things we worry and stress over; in the end, none of it matters. When we meet our Savior face to face, none of it will matter: "The world and its desires pass away, but whoever does the will of God lives forever" (1 John 2:17).

I ponder in my heart, the story of the precious widow in the Bible who gave everything she had out of her poverty. This beautiful woman understood Kingdom finances and ultimately knew who her provider was. She may have been poor in the world's eyes, but she was rich in the Kingdom of God.

> Jesus sat down opposite the place where the offerings were put and watched the crowd putting their money into the temple treasury. Many rich people threw in large amounts. But a poor widow came and put in two very small copper coins, worth only a few cents. Calling His disciples to Him, Jesus said, "Truly I tell you, this poor widow has put more into the treasury than all the others. They all gave out of their wealth; but she, out of her poverty, put in everything—all she had to live on." (Mark 12:41–44)

What does this story teach us? That God sees the heart. Many people were giving money that day. The Scripture says that the rich were throwing in large amounts. The widow's money added up to nothing in the world's eyes, and yet Jesus said she gave more than all the others. She understood Kingdom finances. She knew she could not out-give God. She knew that if she gave all she had her needs would be met. God looks at the heart and this story reveals that He adores a heart of sacrifice.

Let's pray:

Lord, help us to become radical givers. Allow us to view our finances through Your eyes. We are only stewards of the gifts You give to us. Everything we have belongs to You. Let us become conduits of Your blessings to everyone around us. Let us see a need and give without hesitation. Forgive us for being all about us. Help us to understand that as we give we are actually storing up for ourselves treasures in heaven. Matthew 6:19–21 says, "Do not store up for yourselves treasures on earth, where moths and vermin destroy, and where thieves break in and steal. But store up for yourselves treasures in heaven, where moths and vermin do not destroy, and where thieves do not break in and steal. For where your treasure is, there your heart will be also." Help us to understand that life on this earth is very short. Give us hearts that desire to store up treasure in heaven where we will spend eternity with You. Change our mindset. Transform our hearts. In Jesus' name we pray. Amen.

Strategy #11: Tithing

PART III

Launched into Identity, Purpose, and Destiny

CHAPTER 15

Expectation

Here Comes Your Miracle

Trust in the Lord with all your heart
and lean not on your own understanding;
in all your ways submit to Him,
and He will make your paths straight.
Proverbs 3:5–6

Is your faith arising? Are you ready to walk into your own miracle? Is there something you have been contending for? Many of you are living with daily pain. Others can't seem to get free of those binding addictions. Some of you are crying out for your marriage or a lost loved one. Somebody out there is asking, "Who am I and what am I here for?" There is nothing too big for our God. Come to Him with your questions and with expectation. He adores a heart of expectation.

Some of you have received news so devastating that it comes in like a flood, drowning you in a sea of anguish. What should your response be? The old you would allow fear and despair to rise up. The new you opens your Bible to James 1:2–4 where it says, "Consider it pure joy, my brothers, whenever you face trials of many kinds, because you know that the testing of your faith develops perseverance. Let perseverance finish its work so that you may be mature and complete, not lacking anything." Wow! What a scripture! When your world turns upside down, do you choose to believe that God is making you mature and complete, lacking nothing? Or do you wallow and allow the thoughts of the enemy to take over and destroy you? Do you believe and meditate on the Word of God? Or do you let shame, guilt, remorse, and condemnation rush in?

The Lord has been teaching me how mandatory it is for our health and well-being to keep His perspective on things. We need to constantly look at our circumstances from heaven's view. His plans are perfect. His ways are higher. His thoughts are deeper. "No eye has seen, no ear has heard, and no mind has imagined what God has prepared for those who love Him" (1 Corinthians 2:9, BSB). Do I love Him? Yes! With all my heart! Does God love me? Yes! No doubt about that one!

Human nature tells you to dwell on your circumstance. But, God! What does He have to say about it? He says that "All things work together for the good of those who love God, who are called according to His purpose" (Romans 8:28, CSB). Will you choose to believe the Word of the Lord, which has stood the test of time? Or will you choose to allow your emotions, your fears, your doubts, and your unbelief to run rampant and have a heyday in your head? It is at these very moments that you must stand on truth. You must stand on the Word of God, which is not changing, which does not waver in times of devastation and chaos: "God is not human, that He should lie, not a human being, that He should change His mind. Does He speak and then not act? Does He promise and not fulfill?" (Numbers 23:19). God is God and you are not.

It is time to believe that God is who He says He is and that God does what He says He does. God is always true to His Word. He cannot act contrary to His Word. It's time to start seeing yourself walking in the promises of God. Where you see yourself, you will find yourself. See yourself healed. See your marriage restored. See your wayward child running home. See your life of addiction and abuse turn into a hunger and thirst for God alone, for His plans and purposes. See your broken heart of loneliness and depression being filled up with the Holy Spirit as you allow Him to become the lover of your soul. See poverty break off of your life once and for all as you see yourself prosperous. See yourself as victorious, no longer a victim. See yourself as the man or woman walking in the authority that God created you to walk in. It's time to take back your true identity.

Call those things that are not as though they are.

Call those things that are not as though they are (Romans 4:17). We see over and over in the Bible that those who approached Jesus with expectation received their miracle. Read Luke 8:43–48, the story of the woman who pressed through the crowd, knowing that if she could just touch the hem of Jesus' robe she would be instantly healed. She did just that and received her immediate healing. Meditate on the story of the blind man in Luke 18. He cried out to Jesus, knowing if he could just get the attention of the Lord, he would be healed. Everyone told him to be quiet, but he cried out all the louder until he got Jesus' attention and received his healing. Luke 18:27 says, "What is impossible with man is possible with God." Begin believing for the impossible.

In August of 2017 we were preparing to celebrate the marriage of my son and his beloved fiancée. The wedding was to be held in August at a beautiful outdoor venue full of trees with a bubbling brook running through. As the week of the wedding approached, the weather was not looking good for our outdoor event with no indoor back-up plan. Fear began to rise up in my spirit. As I took the fear captive and asked the Lord to replace it with His peace, He reminded me of something that had happened during a prayer meeting a couple of months earlier.

I was praying with a group of women and we were listening to worship music, each one praying silently. I had my eyes closed and felt the gentle touch of a hand upon my shoulder. I opened my eyes to see a beautiful elderly woman in front of me. She opened her mouth and said, "The Lord says, 'I give you command over the wind and the waves, over the elements. You will speak with authority over them.'" I pondered in my heart what had been spoken and was amazed with wonder as to what it could possibly mean. I immediately wrote her words in my journal. I knew that the Lord had authority over the wind and the waves, and I knew that according to the Word of God in John 14:12, we are to do even greater things than Jesus did while He was here on earth. Yet, I was baffled as to what this could possibly mean for my life.

As the day of the wedding approached and there was a ninety-percent chance of rain forecasted, I began to panic, thinking my kids were foolish to not have made other arrangements in case of inclement weather. Their faith was much stronger than mine as they remained calm and unworried. As I began frantically praying, a peace began to sweep over me as the Lord brought to mind that encounter in the prayer room and the words that precious woman had spoken over me. A holy boldness began arising in my spirit. I began remembering stories in the Bible where Jesus had commanded the wind and the waves to stop. At His command, they stopped.

The rain began coming down a half hour before the wedding, as forecasted. People raced into panic mode, covering tables, decorations, etc. I stepped out onto the porch of the house on the property and began boldly commanding the rain to stop, the clouds to disperse, and the sun to shine forth in the name of Jesus. I had reached out to others to join in prayer for the weather and knew many were praying. Within fifteen minutes, the skies had cleared, and the sun was shining brightly over the venue. The groomsmen dried off the chairs as we welcomed the guests. The evening turned out to be the most beautiful wedding I have ever experienced.

As we reminisced the next day, we recounted the evening before the wedding. We were outside for the rehearsal and bugs were flying everywhere. It was annoying and extremely bothersome. In that moment, we realized that God had sent the rain to clean and refresh the atmosphere for this wedding that He had ordained. There was not a bug in sight all evening and the temperature was beautifully pleasant as we celebrated a most gorgeous union in the Lord.

This experience blew my faith through the roof. God had sent a woman, two months ahead of time, to give me a message that would empower me to walk in the authority I carry as a daughter of God. As the fear of rain began to arise, I was reminded of the words she spoke and went into action based on my faith. The rain was actually a gift to get rid of all bugs and pests that we had experienced during the rehearsal. It's all in how we look at things. We can take the enemy's perspective which brings fear and anxiety, or we can take God's perspective which ushers in peace and authority.

Life is not easy. No matter how far we have come, no matter how mature we think we are, there will be triggers. Triggers are things that happen that attempt to knock us back into our old defeatist mindsets and behaviors. For instance, as I've been on my healing journey, I sometimes wake up with an old familiar pain, or a headache, and fear instantly arises. The enemy begins to taunt me with thoughts of, *You're not really healed. Here comes another migraine!* It is crucial at these moments that I immediately take those thoughts captive (2 Corinthians 2:4–5), give them to God, and meditate on His promises and His truth that remind me that *by His stripes I am healed* (Isaiah 53:5).

At times you may get triggered by something someone says that brings up a lie from your past. An immediate offense rises up in your spirit. When this happens, it is of utmost importance that you take up your shield of faith (Ephesians 6:16) which will extinguish every flaming arrow of the enemy. Refuse to be offended.

I have a friend who is attempting to set boundaries in a relationship with her mother that is extremely toxic. She has come very far in transforming her mind in the ways of God. Yet, her mother is still very much a part of her life. She has to take up her shield of faith daily, allowing those arrows (triggers) to bounce off each time her mother speaks damaging, painful remarks. The old emotions, from that broken little girl inside, attempt to rise up to take her back to a place of depression and captivity, but God has given her new tools and strategies. She refuses to get entangled. 2 Timothy 2:4 reminds her to "Share in the suffering as a good soldier of Christ Jesus. To please the recruiter, no one serving as a soldier gets entangled in the concerns of daily life" (HCSB).

The enemy wants nothing more than for you to get "entangled in the concerns of daily life" so that you get off course from your assignments. God has you on assignment.

You can choose to keep your eyes on the bigger picture — why you are here and what were you created to fulfill — or you can constantly be sucked back into the daily entanglements. If Satan can keep you worried about the symptoms you are feeling, the remarks another person makes to you or about you, how you are going to pay the bills this month, how your spouse is not doing what you think he or she ought to be doing, or how your children are making poor choices, then he has accomplished taking you off of your God assignments. The minute these daily entanglements come your way, take them captive, give them to Jesus, and get back to what God has you doing. After all, can't He do a much better job with your spouse and your children than you possibly can? Isn't He much more able to take care of your pain, injury, or illness than you are? Isn't He much more capable of dealing with your finances than you are? If you believe that He is your healer, your provider, your deliverer, your protector, and your Father who loves you, then let go and give Him your concerns so that you can get on with the more important things, your God assignments, that will change the world.

I had a dream recently where I was sitting on a couch in a house, looking out a sliding glass door. There was a rattlesnake wrapped around my neck. I sat in silence, completely paralyzed by fear, not moving an inch. His rattle was going off full force and I knew death was staring me in the face. There was no escape. My husband entered the room and immediately saw the sheer terror in my eyes. He ran over to me and, without hesitation, grabbed the snake by the head, yanked it off of me, and threw it out the door.

I woke up from the dream, heart pounding, amazed at what God revealed. He wanted me to really understand that this is the kind of authority we walk in. The enemy may come in and wrap himself around us, entrap us, and paralyze us in fear and captivity, but all we have to do is grab him by the head and throw him out the door! In the dream, my husband exemplified the authority that we carry as children of God. He did not hesitate. He did not stop or feel helpless thinking, *Oh, no, what should I do?* He did not allow fear to paralyze him. He immediately acted in the authority he carries as a son of the living God and went after the enemy, saving his wife from certain doom. The Word of God promises in 2 Timothy 1:7, "For God has not given us the spirit of fear; but of power, and of love, and of a sound mind" (King James 2000). If you do find yourself experiencing fear as I was in the dream, engage someone to help you, or simply call out the name of Jesus. There is power in His name.

Jesus says in Luke 10:19, "I have given you authority to trample on snakes and scorpions and to overcome all the power of the enemy; nothing will harm you." We know that snakes in the Bible refer to the devil himself; the scorpions represent his little demons that work with him. But, what does the Word say? You have

> *Begin today to take authority over your overwhelming circumstance*

been given power to trample on them and to overcome *all* the power of the enemy! In the dream, my husband didn't pause, waver, or flinch. He operated in this power and moved into action, knowing that nothing would be able to harm him. That is the power that the Lord has intended you to walk in. Begin today to take authority over your overwhelming circumstance and watch God move in power and might.

Pray with me:

Lord, I decree that no weapon formed against me shall prosper (Isaiah 54:17). I come to You with bold faith, knowing that You are for me, not against me. Thank You, Lord, that as I bow to You, my fears melt away. I come to You with expectation, believing that You will have Your way in my health, my finances, my family, my identity, and in all of my overwhelming circumstances. You are God and I am not. Thank You that You are transforming my heart and mind and are shaping me into the world-changer You have destined me to become. Thank You that as I die to myself and I live for You, You are establishing my true identity. In Jesus' name I pray. Amen.

CHAPTER 16

Living the Dream

Purpose, Passion, and Destiny Restored

For nothing will be impossible with God.
Luke 1:37, ESV

A couple of months ago I was in a meeting in a city an hour from home. I left the meeting and texted my husband, Bill, letting him know I would be home in an hour. He responded for me to stop by the city where he was working. He was finishing up a meeting, and suggested we have lunch together. We met at a specific restaurant. As we walked in, the hostess greeted us. She could have taken us to the room on the left or the room on the right. She chose the room on the right, walked us past about ten empty booths, and sat us at a table near three gentlemen.

As we were deciding what to order, I felt a tugging in my spirit that I was supposed to get up and go bless one of the men. I said to my husband, "Honey, I think I'm supposed to go over and bless that man with his back to us." He responded, "Okay! I'll meet you in the car!" After a good chuckle he said, "How about we eat our lunch and when we finish, if you are still feeling it, I'll go over there with you and we can bless him together."

We ate our lunch and I was still feeling it. We got up and walked over to them. I was nervous, not really knowing what I was going to say. I only knew I was to bless him and tell him the Lord loved him. When we got to their table I said, "Hi my name is Debbie, and this is my husband, Bill." Then I looked straight into the man's eyes and said, "I felt the Lord telling me to come over here to let you how much He loves you and that He is passionately pursuing you."

The other men's jaws about hit the floor! Bill and I gave each other a nervous glance. One of the men spoke up, pointing to the man I had spoken to and said, "This man has just been released from prison. I am his friend and (motioning to the other gentleman said), this is his probation officer. We had just been sharing with him about Jesus, telling him how much God loved him and that Jesus had died for his sins. I had just said, 'If what we are telling you is true, God is going to send someone to confirm what we are saying to you.'" It was minutes later

> "The Lord directs the steps of the godly. He delights in every detail of their lives"

that Bill and I walked up to their table and told him how much God loved him. They were blown out of the water. We were blown out of the water. We asked if we could pray for them. Bill prayed over them. Then they prayed over us. The waitress came over to tell us how blessed she was as the ripple effect was going out through the whole restaurant. It was this joyous, amazing moment in time. The beauty is that God truly was passionately pursuing this man who had just been released from prison. He now knows without a doubt that his Father in heaven loves him.

I was so overcome by the love of God. I had been meditating on Psalm 37:23 that week. It says, "The Lord directs the steps of the godly. He delights in every detail of their lives" (NLT). As I got in the car and was praising God for His faithfulness and for how much He loves this man, I was thinking about that verse and how God was orchestrating the whole thing — each and every detail. Bill and I didn't wake up that morning planning to have lunch together. I happened to get out of my meeting. I texted him. He happened to be getting out of his meeting and encouraged me to stop by to have lunch with him. We chose a particular restaurant. The hostess chose which room to lead us to. She chose a particular booth in which to seat us. The Lord prompted my spirit to talk to the man. Bill suggested we wait until after we finished eating. Had we gone when I originally wanted to, the friend would not yet have said that God was going to send somebody to confirm what they were telling him about Jesus. It was incredible how God was orchestrating each of our steps to bless this child of His that had been given a fresh start in life.

I want to encourage you when you feel that gnawing in your stomach, or when God highlights somebody to you, just go up to them even if you don't know what to say. God is so faithful. If you open your mouth and take a baby step, He is going to fill it with a blessing, a word of comfort, or a word of encouragement or exhortation, because that's who He is and that's what He does. That is God's heart. He longs to use each of you to bring hope, joy, and love to this world.

Are you ready to begin walking out your life with purpose and passion? Are you ready to walk in peace and joy? Today is the first day of the rest of your life. Take the plunge and watch what God wants to do with a life surrendered to His biblical blueprint. Begin today to implement these timeless strategies that lead to a life of abundant fulfillment. This is not a set of rules to follow. This is not a religion. This is partnering with the Holy Spirit to fulfill the call and the destiny you were personally created for. This is about an exciting journey that only you and God can fulfill together as you choose to partner with Him.

Acts 17:26–28 in The Passion Translation reads, "He sets the boundaries of people and nations, determining their appointed times in history… it is through Him that we live and function and have our identity." Did you comprehend that? This is *your* appointed time in history! Only *you* can fulfill the plans and purposes for your individual life in this time and season. So many times in life I have looked at others and thought, *I wish I could sing like her*, or *I wish I could write like him*, or *I wish I looked like her,* etc., etc., etc. God wants you to know that He created *you* to be *you* and no one else. He wants you to stop wishing you were somebody else, begin to recognize and appreciate your unique footprint in time, and begin living the life you were created to live.

Meditate on Psalm 37:23, which says that God is ordering your very steps, and get this truth engrained in your soul. If your steps are truly being directed by the Lord, then when you get that phone call with the devastating news, or when you find yourself delayed in traffic, or when you don't get that promotion, or when that family member betrays you, you will be able to say, "Thank You, Lord, that my steps are being directed by You and that absolutely nothing can get in the way of that." As your heart becomes thankful instead of stressed, disappointed, angry, or irritated, you will be able to rest in His promises, knowing He has your best interest at heart. I decree over you Psalm 119:165, "Abundant peace belongs to those who love Your instruction, nothing can make them stumble" (BSB).

There is one main key that I was missing my first thirty years of following Jesus. Though I had accepted Christ as my Lord and Savior at eighteen years old, and had been water baptized, I had not received the baptism of the Holy Spirit. I was missing the key ingredient to living a life of obedience that only comes through the power of the Holy Spirit. In his book, *Smith Wigglesworth Devotional*, Wigglesworth writes:

> After the Holy Spirit comes upon you, you will have power. God will mightily move within your life; the power of the Holy Spirit will overshadow you, inwardly moving you until you know there is a divine plan different from anything that you have had in your life before.[1]

I had been a believer for over thirty years, but I struggled, constantly trying to live a life of obedience, righteousness, and the fullness of God, only to fail over and over again. I wanted to experience the power and authority I read about daily in the Bible, but kept failing, never seeing any substantial fruit. I couldn't seem to hear God or feel His presence. It wasn't until I was baptized in the Holy Spirit that sin didn't come so easily, obedience came in pleasure not in striving, and I began walking out the Gospel in faith, power, and authority.

My prayer for you today is that the Holy Spirit falls on you and transforms you into the person you were created to be. I decree over you that *you* are a world-changer! You did not pick up this book by accident. You are not reading these words by chance. This is a divine appointment, set up for this time and place in your life by a Father who adores you and is passionately pursuing you. His heart is *for* you. He is orchestrating the season you have been waiting for. He longs to fulfill all the plans and purposes He wrote in His book of life from the beginning of time. I know without a doubt that these words are resonating in your spirit as you read them. Your body wants to jump up and down and do a happy dance. Go ahead! God is aligning you with the destiny you were created to fulfill. Decree out loud:

You saw me before I was born.
    Every day of my life was recorded in Your book.
Every moment was laid out
    before a single day had passed. (Psalm 139:16, NLT)

It's hard to believe that I had spent most of my life living in fear. I knew deep down I was created for more, but I felt it was me who had to make it happen. As a college student I had surrendered my life to Jesus, but I found myself still striving. I knew there were morals and things to embrace that led to a healthy and fulfilling life, but I couldn't seem to make it happen or do everything I thought I was supposed to do. I found myself failing over and over again. I walked further and further into illness as each new diagnosis came my way. I embraced each one, researched them on the internet, and agreed with every word spoken over me.

Eventually, I decided enough was enough; I couldn't do it on my own. It took getting to the place where I had to die to myself. I woke up that fearful day, after the night when I had almost taken my own life, and yelled out to the Lord, "Today is the day that I live or die!" That one statement, that cry out to God, was the beginning of a journey like no other. It has been the most exhilarating, adventurous, emotional, stretching ride of my life, but one I would not trade for anything in the world. I was stripped of me and made alive in God. I found out the key was dying to myself and becoming alive in Him:

> My grace is always more than enough for you, and my power finds its full expression through your weakness. So I will celebrate my weaknesses, for when I'm weak I sense more deeply the mighty power of Christ living in me. So I'm not defeated by my weakness, but delighted! For when I feel my weakness and endure mistreatment — when I'm surrounded with troubles on every side and face persecution because of my love for Christ — I am made yet stronger. For my weakness becomes a portal to God's power. (2 Corinthians 12:9–10, TPT)

His grace is truly all we need. Stop striving! Surrender it all to Him. He knows your heartache. He knows your struggles. He knows your strengths. He knows your failures. He knows your triumphs. He knows you intimately. He longs to become your everything. Surrender today. It is long overdue. You have felt it for some time, but it has been overwhelming, and you don't know how you got to this place. Today is the day of your healing! Today is the day of your deliverance! Today is the day your heart gets filled up to overflowing! Today is the day you choose to never look back! Today you have been set free! Today you walk in victory! Today you walk in health! Today you walk in prosperity! Today you step into your true identity! Today you walk in sweet confidence! Today you walk in soundness of mind! Today is the day of your transformation! Today is a day you will never forget! Mark this day down in your journal and watch God take you to a place you never dreamed possible. Give it all to Him. He will give you back all the years that have been stolen by the schemes of the devil: "So I will restore to you the years that the swarming locust has eaten" (Joel 2:25, NKJV). You will be utterly amazed. Your mind will be blown. Boom! This is a now moment in time. Don't let it pass by! Grab hold and embrace it. This is a personal invitation from your Father God. This is your call to action.

CHAPTER 17

Victory for Life

Your Call to Action

So do not fear, for I am with you; do not be dismayed,
for I am your God.
I will strengthen you and help you;
I will uphold you with my righteous right hand.
Isaiah 41:10

L ive the life you were purposed and designed for. You were made to be you. You were born with desires, dreams, aspirations, and giftings. There are things you are passionate about and things you despise. You have certain tastes and abilities. There is no other face that looks exactly like yours. There is no other personality identical to yours. You are unique to this world. Only you can live the life you were destined to live. Only you can fulfill the purposes you were put on this earth to fulfill. If you don't fulfill them, they will go unfulfilled. Begin today living the life you were created to live. Imitate Paul:

> Brothers and sisters, I do not consider myself yet to have taken hold of it. But one thing I do: Forgetting what is behind and straining toward what is ahead, I press on toward the goal to win the prize for which God has called me heavenward in Christ Jesus. (Philippians 3:13–14)

Forget what lies behind! Don't take your old baggage into this new season. God has given you new luggage to unpack and put on. The only time you will want to look back is if you need to forgive someone or ask someone to forgive you. Otherwise, look forward, pressing on toward that which God has called you!

The Lord's plan for your life is so much bigger than your own. If your dream doesn't scare you, it's not big enough. Dream bigger! You were not put on this earth just to survive and maybe influence a couple of people. You were put here to make a mark. Step in and leave your print! You are here to be a mover and a shaker. You were put here to have significant influence as a child of God, impacting your family, your community, your state, your nation, and even the world.

I decree over you that you will be ten times better in understanding, in knowledge, and in wisdom than everyone around you, just as Daniel and his friends were as they chose to follow the Lord. I decree that you will have dreams and visions straight from heaven so that you will know what to do as you face future situations and decisions.

Decree with me:

- I am a son/daughter of the living God.

- I am an heir to the throne, and with that comes all privilege and blessing.

- I walk under an open heaven.

- Jesus died for my sins.

- I repent and choose to walk into a life of righteousness.

- I surrender trying to do it my way.

- I choose to partner with the King of kings and Lord of lords.

- I am excited for this new adventure that begins today.

- I decree that no weapon formed against me and my family will prosper.

- I decree that when the enemy comes in like a flood, the Spirit of the Lord raises up a standard against him.

- I decree that I have been given power and authority to trample upon serpents and scorpions and over all the power of the enemy, and nothing shall harm me or my family.

- I decree that I walk in the power and the authority of Jesus Christ.

- I decree that with that power and authority comes my healing.

- I decree that with that power and authority comes freedom from all addictions.

- I decree that with that power and authority comes the overwhelming love that fills up every lonely and broken place in my heart.

- I decree that the blood of Jesus Christ has broken off all shame, guilt, and despair.

- I decree that the blood of Jesus has broken off all depression and oppression from my life.

- I decree that Jesus is Lord over my finances and that everything I own belongs to Him.

- I decree that my marriage is a covenant made between me, my spouse, and God, and that nothing is allowed to destroy this covenant.

- I decree that my children will live out the full call and destiny of their lives and I plead the blood of Jesus over them.

- I decree that I am a child of the living God and with that comes full identity.

- I decree that I am a powerful, anointed man / woman of God.

- I decree that I know who I am and that I was created with purpose.

- I break off of my life and my family bloodline all generational sin and curses in the name of Jesus.

- I decree that my family is blessed to the thousandth generation.

- I decree that as a child of God, I walk in signs, miracles, and wonders.

- I decree that the Holy Spirit living in me shifts the atmosphere of every place that I walk into.

- I decree that I walk in divine health and prosperity.

- I decree that I only hear the voice of God and that He alone directs my every move.

- I decree that in Him alone do I live and move and breathe.

- I decree that I am filled with passion and purpose.

- I decree that nothing will get in the way of me living out every page written by God in His book of my life.

- I decree that from this day forward every page of my story in the book of life is filled with vibrancy, color, hope, peace, righteousness, favor, and joy.

- I decree that I exercise and walk in every fruit of the Spirit; love, joy, peace, patience, kindness, goodness, faithfulness, gentleness, and self-control.

- I decree that the fullness of the Lord encompasses me.

- I decree that I am His and He is mine.

- I decree there is no other God in my life.

- I surrender all.

- I take up my cross and follow Him.

- I decree that I have been changed from the inside out and I walk in wholeness and soundness of mind.

- I decree that in my weakness I am made strong.

- I die to myself and become alive in Him.

- I decree that today is the first day of the rest of my life.

You are walking into new miracles. Your debt is being cancelled. Your healing is manifesting. Your addictions have been broken. New disciplines and mindsets are beginning to reshape your character. Press into the Word of God and insert your name in the scroll. This is who you are. This is what you were made for. This is your moment to shine. This is the culmination of your destiny, aligning with your true identity. Transformation is upon you. You are walking

Rise up in splendor and be radiant, for your light has dawned and Yahweh's glory now streams from you!

into the supernatural life you were created to walk in. All the stuff of your past was training you for this very moment in history. Embrace it and watch what God does in and through you. Say yes today and watch God be who God says He is and do what He says He does.

Hear the words of the prophet Isaiah:

Rise up in splendor and be radiant, for your light has dawned and Yahweh's glory now streams from you! Look carefully! Darkness blankets the earth, and thick gloom covers the nations, but Yahweh arises upon you and the brightness of His glory appears over you! Nations will be attracted to your radiant light and kings to the sunrise-glory of your new day! Lift up your eyes higher! Look all around you and believe, for your sons are returning from far away and your daughters are being tenderly carried home. Watch as they all gather together, eager to come back to you!

Then you will understand and be radiant. Your heart will be thrilled and swell with joy. The fullness of the sea will flow to you and the wealth of the nations will be transferred to you! (Isaiah 60:1–5, TPT)

I decree over you that "Whether you turn to the right or to the left, your ears will hear a voice behind you saying, 'this is the way; walk in it'" (Isaiah 30:21). You are going to begin hearing the voice of the Lord and you are going to know what to say and what to do in *every* situation. You will be led by the Holy Spirit as you surrender your life and say yes to Him. You are a world-changer! Today is the day you begin living the supernatural life you were destined to live.

My child, never drift off course from these two goals for
your life; to walk in wisdom and to discover discernment.
Don't ever forget how they empower you.
For they strengthen you inside and out
and inspire you to do what is right;
you will be energized and refreshed by the healing they
bring. They give you living hope to guide you,
and not one of life's tests will cause you to stumble.
You will sleep like a baby, safe and sound —
your rest will be sweet and secure.
You will not be subject to terror, for it will not terrify you.
Nor will the disrespectful be able to push you aside,
because God is your confidence in times of crisis,
keeping your heart at rest in every situation.
(Proverbs 3:21–26, TPT)

Now go and partner with the Holy Spirit
to change your world!
And...
To God be ALL the glory!!!

DISCUSSION POINTS

For

Strategies from

Heaven

Discussion Points

Instructions: I encourage you to read this book with a small group of friends for accountability and to experience a deeper impact. It is always powerful to go through life with those who are not afraid to sharpen us, pull us higher, and challenge us to grow.

For best results, be as committed and as candid as possible with your group of trusted friends. Remember to *honor* the code that what is shared in this group, stays in this group.

INTRODUCTION

Knocking on Death's Door

1. In what way(s) do you relate to the doctor's wife?

2. In what way(s) do you relate to the author?

3. Identify your struggle(s). List them in order of severity.

4. What are you hoping to gain from reading this book?

5. Are you willing to commit to walking out your journey with a small group of people for the next 18 weeks? Will you agree to read one chapter per week, answer the questions pertaining to each chapter, and thoughtfully engage in conversation and prayer with this group?

6. Pray with each other for the grace to follow through with this commitment.

CHAPTER 1

Derailed

How did I Get Here?

1. Looking back, are you able to identify how you got into your current situation? Explain.

2. Are you able to recognize the enemy's traps in your situation? Share an example.

3. Identify a person or people that you look to for help when encountering a crisis.

4. Has this person/these people become your "savior" or your wise counsel in place of God? Discuss.

5. Identify something other than a person you have turned to in your time of need (i.e., alcohol, drugs, food, prescription medication, the internet, etc.).

6. What is your view of God? Do you believe He can help you with whatever you are currently facing?

CHAPTER 2

Delivered

Breaking the Chains

1. What are some of the negative mindsets that have carried over from your youth into adulthood? (Ask the Holy Spirit to reveal these to you.)

2. Have you been set free from anything that had you bound? Can you identify specific chains that have been broken?

3. If yes, what did you do with the chains?

4. Do certain things trigger you and bring you back to the painful memories or walk you back into the same crisis over and over again?

5. Is there something that currently has a hold on you that you can't seem to get free from no matter how hard you try? Share with the group.

6. Are you willing to release your situation to Jesus and His finished work of the cross? Pray for each other.

CHAPTER 3

Destined for More

Propel into the Supernatural

1. In what subtle ways has the enemy snuck up on you?

2. Do you recognize that you were made for more?

3. What are some dreams you had as a child or youth that you have allowed to die?

4. Name two tangible steps you can begin to implement to resurrect those dreams.

5. Name one unique gift or talent that you were born with — something God-given.

6. List three things you know you were created for.

CHAPTER 4

The Power of Your Decree

Create the World You've Always Dreamed of

1. In what ways do you identify with Merri's story?

2. Have you spoken something negative and seen it come to pass?

3. What are your thoughts regarding decreeing the Word of God?

4. Name a time when you spoke something positive over your future and it came to pass.

5. In what way does Stuart's testimony bear witness with your spirit?

6. Choose a Bible verse to begin decreeing over your situation. Write it on a notecard to carry with you. Begin memorizing the Scripture, inserting your name where appropriate.

CHAPTER 5

Weapon of Warfare

A Key to Deliverance

1. What is your experience with worship music (hymns, contemporary Christian, gospel, etc.)?

2. Do you have a favorite song that immediately lifts your spirit when you hear it?

3. Go to Youtube.com and type in "Christian Worship Music." Spend some time exploring and listening to different genres. There is literally something for everyone's tastes. Pick out a few songs to have at your immediate disposal when you need to get out of a slump. Share these songs with your group. (A few of my favorite groups are: Jesus Culture, Bethel Worship, Bryan and Katie Torwalt, and Elevation Worship.)

4. Begin to read and meditate on the book of Psalms. David pours out his heart to God in song. Sing through the Psalms putting your own melody to the words. (No excuses! I cannot carry a tune or melody, but in the privacy of my own home, I sing out loud to God. He loves to hear us sing His praise!)

5. Read 2 Chronicles 20:1–30. Discuss as a group.

6. Find a Bible verse that confirms how much God loves to hear you sing praises to His name. Share with the group.

CHAPTER 6

Fiery Arrows

Does God Really Hear Me?

1. Share a time in which God clearly answered one of your prayers.

2. Do you believe that God always answers prayer? Discuss.

3. Have you ever said or believed the phrase, "All we can do is pray"? Has your view of that changed after reading this chapter? In what ways?

4. Do you have something for which you have been praying for a very long time and feel that God is remaining silent on the issue? How does this chapter give you hope to keep contending?

5. Describe a story in the Bible where it seemed God did not answer somebody's prayer, only to find out later that He did.

6. Name a time in your life where God answered your prayer with a totally different solution than you had expected or desired, but the outcome was even better than you had hoped for.

CHAPTER 7

I Can't Understand You!

Revealing the Secret Language

1. Discuss your understanding of praying in tongues.

2. Discuss your experience (positive or negative) with praying in tongues.

3. Discuss the difference between being filled with the Holy Spirit with the evidence of tongues found in Acts 2:4, versus the spiritual gift of tongues in 1 Corinthians 12:8–10.

4. When does speaking in tongues need to be followed by interpretation?

5. What are some benefits of praying in tongues?

6. Why do you feel there is confusion and fear among some believers regarding praying in tongues/praying in the Spirit?

CHAPTER 8

Unlock Your Destiny

The Keys of Thanksgiving

1. Name a hardship you are currently thankful for. Tell why you are thankful in the midst of this trial.

2. Testify about a time where you endured suffering but when it was all said and done you recognized the hand of God in it and became thankful.

3. Share a Bible story that comes to mind where the character was thankful despite his/her circumstances.

4. Some people struggle to have a thankful heart. What are some hindrances to having a heart of gratitude?

5. Is there anything you need to repent of where you found yourself whining and complaining instead of operating with a heart of gratitude? Share how you could have handled the situation better.

6. Spend some time with your group thanking God for the difficult situations you currently find yourselves in. Read James 1:2–4 together and thank God that He is making you mature and complete, lacking nothing.

CHAPTER 9

Wounds of Betrayal

Freedom from the Sting

1. Share an instance in which you were wounded by betrayal.

2. Have you been able to forgive, release, and bless your betrayer(s)? If not, what is holding you back?

3. Are you willing to allow the group to pray for you to release this hold that the enemy has on you? As a group, pray for anyone holding onto unforgiveness or needing deliverance from the pain of betrayal.

4. Name a character in the Bible who was betrayed. How did they handle the betrayal?

5. How do you typically handle offenses?

6. Ask the Lord to reveal any offenses of the heart you may be holding on to. As a group, pray for the Lord to free each of you from offense. Pray together that you would become a people who are not affected or derailed by offense. Take up the shield of faith and determine that all future offense will bounce off of you.

CHAPTER 10

Covered in the Blood

Revelation-Knowledge

1. Did Sheri's story build your faith or stretch you in any way?

2. What is your understanding of the power of the blood of Jesus?

3. Find one Old Testament verse that discusses sacrificing a pure spotless animal to atone for your sins. Find one New Testament verse that discusses how Jesus became the ultimate atonement for your sins. Discuss with the group.

4. Choose a current situation you can begin immediately pleading the blood of Jesus over.

5. Spend some time praying for the Lord to expand your brain capacity to be able to comprehend the immensity of what He did for you, your family, and every crisis you will encounter, when He died on the cross.

6. Take communion together thanking Jesus for what He did on the cross.

CHAPTER 11

Is Your Family Cursed?

Unlock Blessings to the Thousandth Generation

1. Ask the Lord to reveal any generational curses being carried down in your family bloodline. Write them down and share with the group.

2. Ask the Lord to forgive you and your ancestors for all known and unknown generational sins. Write out a prayer of repentance.

3. Ask the Lord to break off all generational curses and to let them end with you.

4. Plead the blood of Jesus over yourself, your children, and your grandchildren. Ask God to bless your family to the thousandth generation per His Word.

5. Search out a couple of Scriptures that speak to you regarding the areas that apply to your circumstance, e.g., health, provision, blessings and favor, protection, wisdom, etc. Write out some decrees, based on these Scriptures, to begin speaking over your family bloodline.

6. Keep track of your words during the day by carrying around a 3"x5" card. On the card write the word "Positive" on one side and "Negative" on the other. Make a tally mark each time you catch yourself saying a positive or negative statement on the appropriate side of the card. When you catch yourself saying a

negative remark, ask the Lord to forgive you and break off the word-curse, then move on with your day. Don't dwell. This will get easier and easier and you will be amazed at the transformation of your mind. Do this a few different times throughout the next several months and watch the miracle God performs in you.

CHAPTER 12

Secret Weapons

Oil and Cloth

1. What is your experience, if any, with anointing oil?

2. What is your experience, if any, with prayer cloths?

3. How do you feel about implementing these strategies for the current situation you are contending for?

4. Share with the group one way you could immediately implement this strategy.

5. Does your church/ministry incorporate the use of anointing oil or prayer cloths? If so, do you have any testimonies to share with the group?

6. Go through your home this week and anoint your windows and doorposts with oil. Walk your property lines anointing your fence posts with oil and decree that only angelic presence is welcome on your property and in your home. Command all demonic influence to go in Jesus' name.

CHAPTER 13

I'm So Hungry

Break Through to Your Victory!

1. What are your views on fasting?

2. Have you ever fasted for something? What was the outcome?

3. Share one failure or one victory with attempting to fast.

4. Read Daniel 1 together with your group. Discuss.

5. What is one thing you would like to fast for in order to see breakthrough?

6. Pray for one another to have the grace to fast.

CHAPTER 14

I Can't Afford to

You Can't Afford Not to!

1. What are your views on tithing?

2. Do you have any fears or inhibitions in regards to tithing? Share with the group.

3. Do you believe there is a difference between tithing in the Old Testament versus New Testament views on giving? Discuss.

4. Do you have a testimony to share with the group regarding tithing?

5. Are you willing to begin giving/tithing if you are not already doing this? If you are already tithing, are you willing to risk giving even more to watch God do the miraculous?

6. Read Galatians 6:7 together. Discuss the concept of reaping and sowing.

CHAPTER 15

Expectation

Here Comes Your Miracle

1. Name one thing you are currently contending for in life.

2. Pray and ask God what He has to say about this issue. Share what He reveals to you.

3. Can you picture the issue the way God sees it?

4. Write out on paper the new vision God is giving you about your situation. Pick out a Bible verse that confirms this vision. Post it around your house — on your refrigerator, your bathroom mirror, your office desk, and other places — to remind you of His truth.

5. Share a couple of strategies from this book that you have begun implementing and the victories that have come.

6. Pray for one another regarding your new vision.

CHAPTER 16

Living the Dream

Purpose, Passion and Destiny Restored

1. Are you ready to make tangible changes to begin walking out your God-given destiny?

2. Name 3 things you have done or would like to implement as a result of reading this book.

3. Share any struggles associated with these changes.

4. Share your victories associated with these changes.

5. What is one thing the Lord convicted you of while reading this book? Did you act on that conviction? If not, why not?

6. Confess any hindrances you are coming up against and give them to God. Have the group pray over you for your breakthrough.

CHAPTER 17

Victory for Life

Your Call to Action

1. Choose some of the decrees in this chapter that apply to you and commit to decreeing them out loud for 30 days.

2. Write out five of your own unique decrees that apply to your situation and begin decreeing those as well.

3. Commit to reading your Bible every day. Start small if you are not in this habit already. Five minutes a day can change your life. Ask the Lord to make you hunger for His Word. Ask Him to bring His Word to life for you as you read and meditate on it.

4. In one short year the author went from being on ten prescription medications per day to zero. What is one major goal you have that you can begin praying in right now?

5. Where did you see yourself before you were sideswiped by the enemy?

6. Can you commit to allowing God to be who He says He is and to do in your life what He already accomplished on the cross? Are you ready to surrender ALL to Him and walk into the unique destiny you were created to fulfill? Pray as a group for each person.

Notes

Chapter 2: Delivered

1. Scriptures to pray over your spouse:

"How blessed is my husband (insert name), who does not walk in the counsel of the wicked, nor stand in the path of sinners, nor sit in the seat of scoffers, but his delight is in the law of the Lord and he meditates on it day and night, and he will be like a tree firmly planted by streams of water which yields its fruit in its season and its leaf does not wither and in whatever he does he prospers." Psalm 1:1–3

"I also pray for (insert name) always that our God would count her worthy of this calling, and fulfill all the good pleasure of His goodness and the work of faith with power." 2 Thessalonians 1:11

"I pray that the God of our Lord Jesus Christ, the Father of glory would give to (insert name) the spirit of wisdom and revelation in the knowledge of him, the eyes of his understanding being enlightened; that he may know what is the hope of his calling, what are the riches of the glory of his inheritance in the saints, and what is the exceeding greatness of his power toward we who believe, according to the working of his mighty power." Ephesians 1:17–19

"May He grant (insert name) according to her heart's desire, and fulfill all her purpose." Psalm 20:4

"My husband (insert name), who is a wise man, will hear and increase learning, and because he is a man of understanding, he will attain wise counsel." Proverbs 1:5

"May (insert name) seek first the kingdom of God and His righteousness, and all these things shall be added to her." Matthew 6:33

"He restores (insert name)'s soul; He leads him in the paths of righteousness for His name's sake." Psalm 23:3

"May (insert name) walk worthy of the calling with which she was called, with all lowliness and gentleness, with long-suffering, bearing with one another in love." Ephesians 4:1–2

"Lord, who may abide in your tabernacle? Who may dwell in your holy hill? (insert name) who walks uprightly, and works righteousness, and speaks the truth in his heart." Psalm 15: 1–2

"My eyes shall be on (insert name), the faithful of the land, that she may dwell with Me; she who walks in a perfect way, she shall serve Me." Psalm 101:6

"The Lord is (insert name)'s rock and his fortress and his deliverer; his God, his strength, in whom he will trust; his shield and the horn of his salvation, his stronghold. (insert name) will call upon the Lord, who is worthy to be praised; so shall he be saved from his enemies." Psalm 18:2–3

2. Stormie Omartian, The Power of a Praying Wife (Eugene, OR: Harvest House Publishers, Inc., 1997).

Chapter 4: The Power of Your Decree

1. Decrees to pray over your loved one:

"And we know that in all things God works for the good of those who love him, who have been called according to his purpose." Romans 8:28

"The righteous cry out and the Lord hears, and delivers them out of all their troubles." Psalm 34:17

"Now the God of all grace, who called you to His eternal glory in Christ Jesus, will personally restore, establish, strengthen and support you after you have suffered a little." 1 Peter 5:10

"Those who trust in the Lord will renew their strength; they will soar on wings like eagles; they will run and not grow weary; they will walk and not faint." Isaiah 40:31

"Then they cried out to the Lord in their trouble; He saved them from their distress. He sent His Word and healed them. He rescued them from the pit." Psalm 107:19–20

"But if the Spirit of Him that raised up Jesus from the dead dwells in you, He that raised up Christ from the dead shall also quicken your mortal bodies by His Spirit that dwells in you." Romans 8:11

"Trust in the Lord with all your heart and lean not on your own understanding. In all your ways acknowledge Him and He will direct your paths." Proverbs 3:5–6

Chapter 5: Weapon of Warfare

1. Jesus Culture, "Defender (Live)," YouTube video, September 4, 2018, https://www.youtube.com/watch?v=BU6Snucpelo.
2. Michael W. Smith, "Surrounded (Fight my Battles)," YouTube video, December 28, 2017, https://www.youtube.com/watch?v=YBl84oZxnJ4.

Chapter 6: Fiery Arrows

1. "Syria, Russia Say over 100 Missiles Fired, Many Intercepted." *The Times of Israel*, The Times of Israel, 14 Apr. 2018, www.timesofisrael.com/moscow-says-over-100-missiles-fired-at-syria-significant-number-intercepted/.

Chapter 7: I Can't Understand You!

1. Pastor Roger Williams, Senior Pastor of CrossRoads Church, Atascadero, CA.
2. *Smith Wigglesworth Devotional* (Kensington, PA: Whitaker House, 1999), 190.

Chapter 8: Unlock Your Destiny

1. *The Boy in the Striped Pajamas*, directed by David Heyman (Miramax, Heyday Films, BBC Films, 2008).

Chapter 10: Covered in the Blood

1. Bill Johnson, "Communion and the Finished Work of the Cross," YouTube video, June 19, 2017, https://www.youtube.com/watch?v=kxXfO_B74kw.
2. Robert Lowry, *Nothing but the Blood of Jesus*, 1876, public domain.

Chapter 11: Is Your Family Cursed?

1. Graeme Walsh, *Generational Sin and Curses* (Thomas Nelson, Inc., 1984), 4. Used by permission.
2. Walsh, 16–17.
3. Suggested reading:

   Vito Rallo, *Breaking Generational Curses and Pulling down Strongholds* (Creation House Press, 2000).

   Marilyn Hickey, *Breaking the Generational Curses: Overcoming the Legacy of Sin in Your Family* (Harrison House, 2001).

   Graeme Walsh, *Christianity and Freemasonry: Are they Compatible?* Self-published, 2015.

Chapter 12: Secret Weapons

1. Joseph Prince, "Understanding the Significance of the olive tree and anointing oil," accessed June 28, 2019. https://www.josephprince.org/blog/articles/understanding-the-significance-of-the-olive-tree-and-anointing-oil.

2. Anointing Oil Recipe: Mix together 8 oz. almond oil, 1 eyedropper full of frankincense, 2 eyedroppers of myrrh, and 4 eyedroppers of cinnamon. This recipe will make a substantial amount that you can pour into small bottles to share with friends.

Chapter 16: Living the Dream

1. *Smith Wigglesworth Devotional,* 153.

About the Author

Debbie Bilek is a miracle in the making! She has been healed of fibromyalgia, chronic fatigue syndrome, Hashimoto's thyroiditis, Sjögren's syndrome, migraine headaches, and reflex sympathetic dystrophy. Her passion is to see people healed, delivered, and restored to their true identity. She speaks the Word of God over lives with power and authority, imparting truth and transformation, fueling them to live out their unique purpose and God-given destiny. Debbie has been married for 32 years to her college sweetheart and the love of her life, Bill. Together they have three grown children who are destined to be world-changers.

Your Next Steps

Congratulations for starting the journey to live out your true call and destiny by implementing these strategies from heaven. Here are some next steps to ensure your success.

1. Get together with a small group of people and work through this book, one chapter per week. Read the chapter at home and answer the questions in the back of the book that pertain to the appropriate chapter. Meet weekly to discuss what you are learning. Share testimonies and struggles, hold each other accountable, and pray for one another.

2. Join the *Strategies from Heaven* online coaching series for further mentoring opportunities. Register at: StrategiesFromHeaven.com

Printed in Great Britain
by Amazon